PETER JACKSON

# The Transformations of Helen

## Indo-European Myth and the Roots of the Trojan Cycle

Münchener Studien zur Sprachwissenschaft
Herausgegeben von Norbert Oettinger und Eva Tichy

Beiheft 23, Neue Folge

Peter Jackson

# THE TRANSFORMATIONS OF HELEN

## INDO-EUROPEAN MYTH AND THE ROOTS OF THE TROJAN CYCLE



J.H. Röll

**Bibliographische Information Der Deutschen Bibliothek**
Die Deutsche Bibliothek verzeichnet diese Publikation in
Der Deutschen Nationalbibliographie;
detaillierte bibliographische Daten sind im Internet über
http://dnb.ddb.de abrufbar.


Gedruckt auf chlorfreiem, alterungsbeständigem Papier.
Gesamtherstellung: Verlag J.H. Röll GmbH

Printed in Germany
ISSN 0580-1354
ISBN 10: 3-89754-260-9
ISBN 13: 978-3-89754-260-0

TABLE OF CONTENTS

Acknowledgements .................... 7

I. INTRODUCTION .................... 9
The Prehistory of Greek Mythology and Poetics .................... 11
The Indo-European Heritage .................... 11
The "Cyclic" Tradition .................... 25

II. FATHER HEAVEN, HEAVEN'S DAUGHTER,
AND THE DIVINE TWINS .................... 33
The Rape of Nemesis .................... 34
Shape-shifting, Rape, and χορός .................... 42
The Spartan Dawn .................... 48
Heaven's Incest .................... 56
The Story of Saraṇyū .................... 72
Helen and Saraṇyū, εἴδωλον and *sávarṇa* .................... 84

III. RETURNING HEROES .................... 95
Nestor, **nes*, and the Nāsatyas .................... 96
The Dioscuri as Rescuers at Sea .................... 100
The Story of Bhujyu and Indo-Iranian Rescue *epyllia* .................... 103

IV. EPILOGUE: THE ROOTS OF THE TROJAN CYCLE .................... 111
Abbreviations .................... 119
Bibliography .................... 123
Index of Passages .................... 131
Index of Words .................... 135

## ACKNOWLEDGEMENTS

Despite its modest size, this study has gone through many phases and revisions over a period of at least six years. What began as the draft of a short paper, compiled in the Summer of 2000, finally ended up as a monograph.

It is my pleasant task to acknowledge a group of excellent scholars who helped this study improve considerably. First of all I would like to thank Norbert Oettinger, without whose support and scholarly advice this study would never have been pursued in the first place. It was one of his seminars in the Spring of 2000 that first turned my attention to the issues treated in this book. In his capacity as co-editor, Norbert Oettinger also encouraged me to submit the manuscript for publication in the MSS Monograph Series. Among the other scholars associated with the Department of Indo-European Linguistics at the University of Erlangen-Nürnberg, where I was fortunate to spend a year as Alexander von Humboldt-fellow, I owe particular thanks to Manfred Brust. Our discussions over the last six years have encouraged me to strike the golden mean between pedantry and sheer speculation that makes philology worth pursuing. Furthermore, I am indebted to Berhard Forssmann and Robert Plath for offering careful and critical input on two early versions of this study.

Stephanie Jamison has probably spent more time commenting on the linguistic and philological details of this study than anyone else. While I regret my failure to meet all her critical points with equivalent accuracy, I still wish to emphasize my sincere gratitude for her painstaking work. From my standpoint as a student of religion, her approach to Vedic and other Indo-European texts will always stand out as the ultimate recipe for major breakthroughs in comparative mythology.

I prepared the final versions of the three major sections of this study as a junior fellow at Harvard's Center for Hellenic Studies (Washington D.C.) during the academic year 2002/2003. I am deeply indebted to the helpful staff, as well as to the other junior fellows, for contributing to the stimulating atmosphere in the Center's wonderful facilities. A very special thanks goes to Gregory Nagy and Douglas Frame. They both commented on crucial issues of my work in progress and shared with me their ingenious takes on Greek and Indo-European mythology in an open-minded and inspiring manner.

The final preparation of the manuscript was undertaken at my current place of work, the Department for Religious Studies at the University of Tromsø. I wish to thank my colleagues and students at the department for their willingness to engage in discussions of general theoretical and methodological interest. I am also thankful to Synnøve des Bouvrie at the Classics Department for many inspiring conversations during the last years. The Research Counclil of Norway, as well as two anonymous readers engaged by the Council, are acknowledged with gratitude for complying with my application for a large publication grant. I also wish to thank the editors at Verlag Dr. J. H. Röll for preparing my manuscript for the press. Last but not least, I address my sincere gratitude to Jill Wolfe at the English Department for revising my English and for offering many helpful suggestions on matters of clarity.

Needless to say, none of the persons mentioned above should be held responsible for any inaccuracies that still remain in this book.

Peter Jackson
Tromsø, September 2006

# I. INTRODUCTION

It would be both wrong and dubious to address issues of roots and origins without reservation. These issues evoke the notion of absolute beginnings, which is a matter of metaphysics rather than of history and philology. By "roots" in this connection, however, I merely refer to conditions that cannot be made explicit without the aid of comparative evidence. Instead of being regarded as something absolute, beginnings and origins could also be understood as the current closure of historical vision and as points of subdivision in a genealogical ramification.

The present study endeavours to apply these radical concerns within the area of mythology. Nevertheless, it should be pointed out that any attempt to trace the origin of a myth by merely examining its plot is bound to fail. What one may succeed in doing, on the other hand, is tracking down early versions of a myth, as well as early connotations of themes and agents, by paying attention to the tradition of their performance. Tellers of myth are particularly dependent on performative prescriptions since they address groups in the present with a real or pretended message from the past, often explicitly urging these groups (or representatives of these groups) to pass down the myth to future generations in an unaltered state. An effective method of safeguarding the transmission of such messages is to encode them in poetic diction. This encoding implies a conventional modification (or even deformation) of everyday language, which need not be restricted to merely aesthetic purposes. By exaggerating the segmentation and intonation of spoken discourse, introducing rhymes, alliterations or circumlocutions, a verbal message is created that is both easy to recognize and easy to recall, but not necessarily easy to understand. Even though this laborious encoding and decoding of poetic messages has to make sense to the parties involved, the meaning of the message tends to be much more sensitive to change than the means by which it is encoded. Thus it is only when we have access to such messages belonging to different yet once related traditions that we may hope to recover earlier strata of the plot.

I have so far alluded to myth as an unambiguous category. It is surely not. In view of the various and dissonant attempts to define myth during the last decades, I am only ready to make a few assumptions as to the general expectations of such a definition. Myth should not, I believe, be defined in terms of its content. It may be *about* virtually anything. A myth should rather be defined in terms of the means and circumstances of its performance. The persistency in defining myth with reference to content is due to the fact that such means and circumstances have become associated with certain types of stories, not because the content dictates such circumstances. These stories have to acquire a certain social priority, they have to be articulated and handed down through generations, before it makes any sense to treat them as myths. Furthermore, myths are not always narratives in the sense that they present a consistent course of events. They may in fact be highly allusive and unaffected by narrative time.

The stories discussed in the following chapters are neither strikingly similar on the surface nor can they be restored to a single version. Belonging to different societies, told and performed for a variety reasons, they were altered and extended, abandoned and recovered. Nevertheless, it is their common oral traits that shall concern us here. These traits lie embedded in the names and epithets of the agents, in the proximity of these names and agents, and in the words and phrases with which these agents are associated. Perhaps, it is the performative priority assigned to such traits that allow us to recognize the stories as myths. If these traits can be shown to form parts of a larger whole, they will at once provide insights into a textual heritage reaching far beyond the traditions compared.

## *The Prehistory of Greek Mythology and Poetics*

The first extensive literary remains of the West, the *Iliad* and the *Odyssey* owe a lot of their purported magnificence to factors that precede the present structure of the poems as well as those who first performed them. First we might consider reflexes of historical events, places, and persons in the tradition of the Trojan War, particularly those belonging to Bronze Age Aegean, despite how little of this historical past that actually survived the force of epic imagination. We should then consider the importance of an already established tradition of the Trojan War predating the evolution and composition of the Homeric poems. This tradition is reflected by the early visual arts, by the poems of the Epic Cycle, and by the lyric of the Archaic Age. The possibility of Near Eastern and other external literary influences on the Homeric poems should also be taken into consideration. And last, but not least, we must consider aspects of a poetic and mythical heritage in early Greek society that were not restricted to the Hellenic tribes, but rather belonged to a much older Indo-European tradition. In this chapter, I shall pay particular attention to the last issue, because it is the existence and enactment of Indo-European components in Greek poetry that condition this study.

## *The Indo-European Heritage*

A suitable starting point is to consider the very notion of the poet and his craft in Greek society. The poems of Pindar supply an excellent context in this regard. While referring to the epic past, Pindar employs specific traditional images in order to situate himself in a tradition of poetic performance. Having described the killing of Memnon, for instance, Pindar claims (*Nem.* 6, 53-54) that the older poets found a "highway" (ὁδὸν ἀμαξιτόν) in such deeds, and that he has made this road his "own concern" (αὐτὸς μελέταν) by following along.[1] This image, which illustrates the inner conflict of traditional composition-in-performance, applies particularly well to Pindar: a poet who, on the one hand, is called to account for something new and original while still, on the other hand, having to rely on time-honored conventions in doing so. Whereas we would expect at least *this* image to be a circumstantial invention, it could in fact be assigned to traditional imagery. The topic has been studied by Marcello Durante, who gave numerous examples of metaphors for speech as a "path" in Vedic, Avestan, and Greek.[2] Consider the following stanza of a Vedic hymn addressed to the god Soma (9,91,5ab): "as of old [...] *prepare the paths* (*patháḥ kr̥ṇuhi*) *for a new song* (*návyase* [...] *sūktā́ya*)!" The emphasis on the "newness" of a hymn is not an isolated comparandum in Pindar (*Isṭh.* 5, 63: νέον ... ὕμνον). It could even be combined with the image of the "path of verses" in *Ol.* 9, 47-49: "awaken for them a clear sounding *path of verses* (ἐπέων [...] οἶμον); praise wine that is old, but the blooms of hymns that are *newer* (νεωτέρων)."[3] If Durante was correct in regarding this image as the residue of a shared poetic heritage, then Pindar's way of expressing his own relation to the epic past was in itself dependent on a traditional metaphor.

From an Indo-European perspective, this metaphor opens up a whole set of interrelated concepts. A still discernible trace of those who originally prepared this path, the "track of the word," incites the poet to become a path-finder.[4] Furthermore, the poem itself is com-

---

1 To judge from another passage in Pindar (*Pyth.* 4,246-248), ἀμαξιτός seems to denote a more lengthy exposition as opposed to the shorter (but perhaps more challenging) οἶμος.

2 Durante 1968 (= 1958): 242-260, see especially p. 245.

3 Tr. Race 1997: 153.

4 Durante 1968 (= 1958): 244.

pared to a vehicle (preferably a chariot) in which the poet travels (cf. RV 2,31,1-4 and *Ol.* 1,110-111),[5] and the very composition of poetry is compared to the construction of such a vehicle. It was in this context that James Darmesteter first recognized what he referred to as an Indo-European "grammatical metaphor," namely the description of poetry as a skill comparable to the skill of a craftsman.[6] A good example is RV 5,2,11: "for you (Agni) *I have manufactured* (*atakṣam*) this *praise poem* (*stómaṃ*) *as a chariot/wheel* (*ráthaṃ ná*)." Darmesteter noticed that this figure could involve a number of synonyms for the spoken word, one of which (*vácas-*[7]) is also attested in an Avestan compound (*vacastašti-*) serving as a technical term for "strophe" yet with the faded literal sense "word-crafting." Darmesteter could also show that the Greeks used the same figure in their poetry.

Once more favoring deep-rooted metaphors, Pindar describes his predecessors, the epic poets of the past, as the "craftsmen of verses" (ἐπέων τέκτονες) (*Pyth.* 3, 112-114: Νέστορα καὶ Λύκιον Σαρπηδόν [...] ἐξ ἐπέων κελαδεννῶν, τέκτονες οἷα σοφοί / ἅρμοσαν, γινώσκομεν "we know of Nestor and the Lykian Sarpedon [...] from such sounding verses as wise craftsmen *joined together*[8]"). A similar example is found in Pausanias (10,5,8), who preserves a verse concerning the mythical poet Olenus (the supposed founder of oracular hexameter poetry): [...] ἐπέων τεκτάνατ' ἀοιδάν "he fashioned a song out of verses." These etymological matches as to both noun (Ved. *vácas-*, Av. *vacah-*, Gr. [Ϝ]έπος) and verbal root (Ved. *√takṣ,*

5 Durante 1968 (= 1958): 252f.

6 Darmesteter 1878 (= 1968): 116-118.

7 *vácāṃsy ā́śā́* [...] *takṣam* "with my lips have I crafted the words" (RV 6,32,1d).

8 Note that the verb ἁρμόζω was closely associated with the chariot (ἅρμα) among the Greeks from an early date onwards (cf. the Myceanean word *(h)armo-* "wheel").

Av. √*taš*, Gr. √*τεκτ*) suggest the existence of a hereditary formula **u̯ékʷos √*tetḱ* (√**teḱþ*).

Darmesteter's insight is crucial to understanding Indo-European poetics, because the formula simultaneously proves to be a part of the common poetic repertoire and a poetic designation of the action producing the repertoire. It is significant that metaphors of this kind are less pronounced in epic poetry. This could simply be due to characteristics of the epic genre. Pindar's *Epinicians* and the Vedic hymns would thus have more in common, because they were intended as praise poetry, celebrating the appearance and activity of particular individuals (men or gods) at a given point in time (a festival or a sacrificial rite). Since this poetry, as opposed to epic poetry, was more concerned with the situation of its performance, it gave the poet an opportunity to be more of a presence in his own creation. Nevertheless, striking examples in Homeric poetry surface in a set of phraseological and stylistic features that seem less restricted to a particular genre, but which still seem to have constituted the archaic components of oral composition. Verbal and conceptual parallels regarding the notion of lasting fame are particularly widespread. In the wake of Adalbert Kuhn's famous Graeco-Aryan equation κλέος ἄφθιτον = *ákṣiti śrávaḥ, śrávo* [...] *ákṣitam* (**ḱléu̯os ńdgʷhitom)* "imperishable fame," a number of closely related formulas have been identified: *fame* (**ḱléu̯os*) can be associated with eternity and lifetime, it can be *immortal, great, broad*, etc.[9] The concept of lasting fame is also found in proper nouns such as the Mycenean woman's name *a-qi-ti-ta* (*Akʷhthitā*), which must be based on the compound name **Akʷhthitoklewejja*.[10] Another example is the early Germanic man's name *HlewagastiR* "having famous guests" or "fame's guest." The Greek name Κλεόξενος clearly matches the first element of the Ger-

---

9 Schmitt 1967: 61-102. For a more recent treatment of the formula, see Watkins 1995: 173-178.

10 Risch 1987: 3-11.

manic name and corresponds (at least semantically) to the second element.[11] Attention has also been paid to the poetic characterization of horses and chariots: the horses have golden manes, they are swift, prize-winning, and strong-hoofed; the chariots are well-wheeled or well-running, they have golden seats and golden reins.[12]

Parallels of a slightly different kind are found in Hesiod. These may indicate that early gnomic poetry became a vehicle of mythical motifs and religious beliefs reflecting a different stratum of tradition than the one displayed in the Homeric poems. Quite remarkable is the triadic formula (*Op.* 514-16): διάησι [...] / διὰ [...] ἔρχεται / δι' [...] ἄησι [...]. This might be a distorted variant of a climactic formula (*διάησι [...] / δι' [...] ἄησι [...] / διὰ [...] ἔρχεται), which seems to preserve the features of an obsolete myth or a sexual metaphor also attested in Vedic and Hittite. Similar climactic formulas are associated with the same collocation of concepts.[13] Another striking case is the encapsulation of the tabu "not *to urinate standing up* when facing the sun" (*Op.* 727) in the Hesiodic formula ὀρθὸς ὀμείχειν, which is strongly reminiscent of a Vedic phrase attested in a similar context: *ūrdhvó mekṣyāmi* "I will urinate standing up" (AV 7,10,2). This parallel allows the comparativist to reconstruct an Indo-European formula **u̯r̥Hdhu̯os* √**h₃mei̯ǵh*, as well as to retrieve rudiments of its ominous connotations.

A set of common features have been identified in the phraseology of early Indo-European dialects. It is an altogether different task to reconstruct more complex aspects of culture, such as religion and mythology, even though religious and mythical matters were certainly passed down by means of poetic language. These aspects

---

11 Watkins (1995: 246, 404) sees the zero grade **ghs-* of European **ghos-(ti-)* in Greek ξένος.

12 West 1988: 155.

13 Basic discussion in Watkins 1975, followed up by Jackson 2002a, Oettinger (forthcoming), and Watkins (forthcoming).

of culture tend to be much more sensible to change and dissolution, partly because they are more complex, but partly also because they play such an active role in the incorporation, interpretation, and redrafting of the real or imagined legacy that helps to define a society. With a few prominent but far from undisputed exceptions, most Indo-Europeanists confine themselves to identifying some rare but significant cases of persistence in the use of divine names and the verbal tags with which these names were associated. Although these links may offer insights into the prehistoric Indo-European traditions inherited and processed by documented societies, they are rarely taken to constitute more than assemblages of static facts. It would thus be desirable to find a middle course between a linguistic approach that does not seek to clarify the pragmatics of religious vocabulary, and a systematic, textual investigation that largely ignores the linguistic and poetic substance of religious texts.

Historians of religions and anthropologists have readily applied theories of synchronic linguistics in their attempts to describe and understand religious phenomena such as myth (e.g. Lévi-Strauss) and ritual (e.g. Lawson/McCauley). These attempts are informed by the idea that the rules governing human language also operate on other levels of social life. Ferdinand de Saussure, one of the first scholars to make this observation from the point of view of linguistics, would also have insisted that language, just as any other social phenomenon, has a history. Linguistics should thus ideally involve the appreciation of both the synchronic and diachronic dimensions of language. We must assume that language, from the point of view of religious studies, does more than just mediate religious notions as they appear in texts or in spoken discourse, or to serve as a pattern for the description of religion as a synchronic system. In its capacity as a major vehicle of religious notions, language also contains the ruins of its own past. When such aspects of language and culture are approached by Indo-Europeanists, the procedure is sometimes referred to as "comparative (Indo-European) philology" in lieu of a more technical and less philologically oriented "comparative (Indo-European) linguistics." I am advocating here that the study of Indo-European myth should be considered a subdivision of comparative philology. Since this study of myth brings special attention to the linguistic and poetic substance of mythical texts, I refer to it as the study of "Indo-Eurpean myth and poetics" or "Indo-European mythopoetics."[14] Let us take a closer look at the conditions and present status of this a study.

The name "Zeus" is a well-known and indisputable specimen of Indo-European heritage in Greek religion.[15] The Greeks, while regarding this god as the *pater familias* of the divine household, addressed him as πατήρ (most frequently in the vocative Ζεῦ πάτερ "O Father Zeus!"). The same usage is attested in Vedic, where the cognate name *Dyáus* (vocative *Dyàus* [pronounced as a disyllable *díaus*]) is followed by the corresponding epithet *pitár* "father" (cf. AV 6,4,3c). This vocative usage was evidently generalized in some dialects. The terms in Latin *Iuppiter,* Umbrian *Iupater*, and "Illyrian" Δειπάτυρος can only be explained as early derivations from the vocative _*di̯éu̯ ph$_2$tér_. Calvert Watkins has also pointed to reflexes of a similar epithet in Old Irish and Hittite, where he considers the Indo-European semantics to be even better preserved.[16]

A hereditary extension of the epithet "father" is also seen in the Vedic, Avestan, and Greek (perhaps also Latin) characterizations of this (or some other) god as "begetter/procreator" (_*ph$_2$tḗr_

14 The term "mythopoetic," which I take to mean the quality of involving both myth and poetry, should not be confused with the term "mythopoeic," which rather involves the creation (cf. Gr. ποιήσις) of myth (usually in poetic or literary language).

15 For a useful etymological survey, see Jochem Schindler, RE, s.v. "Zeus"

16 Watkins 1995: 8.

*génh*$_1$*tōr*).[17] Compare, for instance, RV 4,1,10d: *dyáuṣ pitā́ janitā́*, RV 1,164,33a: *dyáur me pitā́ janitā́*, Y 44,3b: *ząθā patā*, Aeschylus, *Hiket*. 206: ... Ζεὺς δὲ γεννήτωρ, Euripides, *Ion* 136: Φοῖβός μοι γενέτωρ πατήρ, Ennius, *Annales* 120: *o pater, o genitor*.[18] The comparison between RV 1,164,33a and Ion 136 deserves particular attention, because (as noticed by Schmitt[19]) the phrases also share the enclitic personal pronoun *me*/μοι. Although Schmitt seems to regard the match as accidental, I would not rule out the possibility that the phrases contain traces of the same cultic formula. The cultic context of the passage in *Ion* is explicit (Ion praying in the temple of Apollo with a laurel broom in his hand), and as far as the Rigveda is concerned such a context must be taken for granted on purely generic grounds. We would thus be dealing with an example of formulaics vaguely reflecting the Indo-European language of prayer: **(di̯éu̯s) moi̯ ph*$_2$*tḗr génh*$_1$*tōr* "Di̯eu̯s/GOD is my father and begetter."

The basic meaning of the verbal root from which the noun **di̯éu̯-* derived was probably "to shine" (as seen in the extended Vedic root √*dyut*). This sense also survives in derivative nouns meaning "heaven" (cf. the meaning of Vedic *dyáus* in certain contexts) or "day" (cf. Latin *diēs*, Armenian *tiw,* or the Greek compounds ἔνδιος "at midday" and εὐδία "fair weather"). We should not take this to imply that the Greeks placed Zeus on an equality with the diurnal sky,[20] nor that the aspects inherent in his name inevitably shed light upon his subsequent role in Greek mythology. There are, however, some characteristic features that could be approached in this manner.

---

17 Schmitt 1967: §290ff.

18 Ennius may simply have adopted a Greek formula, which nevertheless gives a more archaic impression in terms of word order (in accord with Behagel's law) than the attested Greek formulas.

19 Schmitt 1967: §291.

20 But see, as an example of archaism, Democritus (Diels, Fr. 30).

In his capacity as the god who decides human fate, Zeus is idiomatically said to "bring on the day" (ἐπ' ἦμαρ ἄγειν/ἐφ' ἡμέρην ἄγειν). An early example is *Od.* 18,136f.: τοῖος γὰρ νόος ἐστὶν ἐπιχθονίων ἀνθρώπων / οἶον ἐπ' ἦμαρ ἄγῃσι πατὴρ ἀνδρῶν τε θεῶν τε. Another example is found in Archilochus (West, Fr. 131), according to whom the mood of mortals vary "as the day that Zeus brings on" (ὁποίην Ζεὺς ἐφ' ἡμέρην ἄγῃ)."[21] Considering the early date of Archilochus' poetry,[22] it is not necessary to interpret Fr. 131 as an allusion to Homer, and we may consequently regard the two examples as independent manifestations of the same traditional locution.[23] It would thus seem all the more relevant to compare, as Martin West has done,[24] Zeus as the god who "brings on day" with Uranos as the god who "brings on night" (cf. *Theog.* 176: ἦλθε δὲ νύκτ' ἐπάγων μέγας Οὐρανός [...] "and great Uranos came, bringing on night"). These and other examples suggest that the two formulas (or locutions) once shared the same thematic background:

A. *ἐπ' ἦμαρ ἄγων Ζεύς
B. νύκτ' ἐπάγων [...] Οὐρανός (*Theog.* 176)

It is plausible that Zeus and Uranos were once conceived as complementary deities, perhaps even as a pair. Although the Greek material is not comprehensive enough to confirm this hypothesis, a stronger case can be made with reference Indo-Iranian comparisons.

---

21 This notion is echoed in Pindar's famous dictum regarding the "creatures of the day" (ἐπάμεροι) (*Pyth.* 8,95-8,96). Cf. also the English word "ephemeral."

22 The memorial of Glaucus, son of Leptines (SEG 14.565), which has been dated to the late Seventh century, clearly belonged to the Glaucus addressed in Archilochus' poetry.

23 Fowler (1987: 26f.), in his discussion of the parallel, seems to presuppose that either Homer or Archilochus has to provide the original version of the locution.

24 West 1966: 218.

Elsewhere, I have reconsidered the possibility that the Vedic gods Mitra and Varuṇa (often addressed as a pair in the Vedic hymns) retain features that associate them with the diurnal and nocturnal aspects of the sky.[25] According to the *Taittirīya Saṃhitā* (TS 6,4,8), Varuṇa produced the night as opposed to Mitra who produced the day (*mitrau 'har ajana yad varuṇo rātriṃ*).[26] Another noteworthy example is the description of the two gods' association with daily work (AV 9,3,18[27]):

> *íṭasyate ví cr̥tā́myápinahyam aporṇuván*
> *váruṇena sámubjitāṃ mitráḥ prātárvyubjiatu*

> "of thy rush-work I unfasten what was tied on, uncovering: [thee] pressed together by Varuṇa, let Mitra in the morning open out" (Whitney [tr.])

Furthermore, the nocturnal aspects of Varuṇa are clearly hinted at in descriptions of his secret supervision of human action. He wears the night sky as a golden garment, to which his "spies" (*spáśas*) have been attached (RV 1,25,13).[28] Zeus is associated with a similar notion at *Op.* 252-53, but the notion could also have been an early property of Uranos. Not least since he was more intimately asso-

---

25 Jackson 2002b. The hypothesis that Mitra and Varuṇa represent the reflexes of a much older divine pair, subjected to decoding and superposition among the Indo-Iranians, remained a hallmark in Dumézil's theory of bipartite sovereignty. While the shared features of Zeus/Uranos and Mitra/Varuṇa (not least their association with day and night) played an important role in Dumézil's early writings (cf. Dumézil 1948), he seems to have lost interest in the issue after 1948.

26 Other examples, most of which are listed in Dumézil 1948: 90ff., are: TS 2,1,7; 5,6,21; TB 1,7,10,1; AV 9,3,18; 13,3,13; AVP 2,72,2 (= 2,80,2).

27 A similar notion occurs in AV 13,3,13: "This Agni becomes Varuṇa in the evening; in the morning, rising, he becomes Mitra" (Whitney [tr.]).

28 Cf. also the description of Ahura Mazdā (theological counterpart of Varuṇa and possible avatar of Indo-Iranian **u̯aruna*) in Yt. 13,2-3 (Jackson 2002b: 50ff.).

ciated with the starry sky (cf. his frequent epithet ἀστερόεις). A pre-Socratic fragment (Critias, *Sisyphus* 33) refers to the "*star-eyed* frame of the sky" (ἀστερωπὸν οὐρανοῦ δέμας) and a depiction of Uranos on the southern frieze of the Pergamon Altar represents the god with a pair of eyes (possibly owl's eyes) on his wings.[29]

Despite such typological points of agreement, the etymological connection between *váruṇa* and οὐρανός was considered untenable for nearly a century. Jacob Wackernagel's objection against Kretschmer and Solmsen in *Sprachliche Untersuchungen zu Homer*[30] was soon canonized as yet another successful attempt to shatter the illusions of Nineteenth century comparative mythology. The etymology was first seriously reconsidered by George Dunkel, who showed in his Zürich inaugural lecture that the equation in fact may be perfectly sound.[31] He interpreted *váruṇa* as a synchronic continuator of the Vedic stem *varu-* (< PIE **u̯oru-*) "to encompass, cover," surviving with different syllabification (**u̯oru̯-*) in οὐρανός. Regarding similar formations, the nouns *varūtṛ́, várūthā*, and the adjective *varūthía* are notable. The etymology implies qualitative vowel gradation**u̯eruno-/*u̯oruno-* (cf. Ved *ápas/ā́pas*), Greek *ἐρανός/ Aeolic ὀρανός (cf. Greek ἐχυρός/ὀχυρός) (< **u̯eru̯n̥o-, *u̯oru̯n̥o-*). This view is compatible with that of M. Kümmel, who reconstructs a Proto-Indo-European root **u̯er* "aufhalten, (ab)wehren" preserved in Greek and subjected to merger with **u̯el* "einschließen, verhüllen" and **Hu̯er* "stecken" in Indo-Iranian.[32] The two names could thus have been formed on the same verbal root meaning "to cover" and a suffix *-no-* (as in Latin *dominus*) denoting worldly or heavenly dominion. Although Dunkel's interpretation remains conjectural, there are some other matches to support it. He notices himself that

[29] Discussion in Simon 1975: 35.

[30] Wackernagel 1916: 136 A. 1.

[31] Dunkel 1990.

[32] LIV 625f.

the same adjective is used to describe both gods as "wide" (**u̯érH-)* or "wide-looking" (cf. RV 1,25,5bc: *váruṇaṃ* [...] *urucákṣasam* ~ *Op.* 45 [and passim]: οὐρανός εὐρύς). Another conspicuous parallel is left unnoticed by Dunkel. Both gods are said to be (or have) a "firm seat *(*sédos)*" (RV 8,41,9d: *dhruváṃ sádaḥ* ~ *Theog.* 128: ἀσφαλὲς ἕδος).

It is noteworthy that Vedic Dyaus/dyaús and Greek Uranos/οὐρανός apparently underwent the same theological and semantic development (e.g. the relative passivity of the gods and the occasional changeover of the proper nouns to nouns meaning "sky"), especially when we consider the extent to which this weakness is restored by their namesakes. There is consequently no need to be overly pessimistic when it comes to outlining the prehistory of the two gods, because some of the features that were lost or fossilized on the one side of the comparison may still be vital on the other. Furthermore, as we shall see in the following chapter, there is textual evidence for a less passive but often overlooked aspect of Dyaus that would support his conformity with Zeus. In the light of these new data, I would cautiously suggest that Georges Dumézil's old idea concerning Zeus/Uranos as the Greek manifestations of the "two sovereigns" (by the side of such pairs as Mitra/Varuṇa and PGmc. *Tīwaz/Wōðanaz) deserves reconsideration. As long as Dumézil's observation was correct in part, the Greek comparandum can be claimed to contain onomastic features that were only retained in corrupted form elsewhere: the name of the (diurnal) Sky-god as a part of the Germanic pair (*Tīwaz [either **di̯éu̯s* or **dei̯u̯ós* "heavenly, god" → √**di̯éu̯*]) and the name of the nocturnal "coverer" as a part of the Vedic pair. The original pair may thus, as reflected by the Greek evidence, have been **di̯éu̯s* (or **dei̯u̯ós*) and **u̯eruno*.

Students of the Indo-European stratum in Greek myth and epic have often regarded the common origin of Eos and Vedic Uṣas (**$h_2$eu̯sṓs*) (cf. also the Roman and Baltic continuators) as a particularly promising case. From the point of view of classical literature, the etymological match is backed up by important observations regarding phraseology and thematics.[33] Deborah D. Boedeker has convincingly argued that Aphrodite absorbed many characteristic features of the Indo-European Dawn-goddess that would no longer apply to Eos. It is generally assumed that Indo-European *$h_2$eu̯sṓs bore the epithet *diu̯ós dhugh$_2$tér "daughter of Di̯eu̯s," although this epithet need not have been exclusively associated with this goddess. She also had a characteristic smile (√*smei̯), which she seems to have shared with her father (cf. RV 2,4,6d),[34] and the Vedic characterization of her "desire" (*vánas-* [< *u̯énos]) (cf. RV 10,172,1: *ā́ yā́hi vánasā sahá* "come here [Uṣas] with your desire") may provide a clue to the origin of the Latin name *Venus*.[35] Just as in the case of Zeus and Dyaus, there are still some crucial points of thematic (and possibly phrasal) interference that have been overlooked. This may also be true of the much-debated Divine Twins, the Greek Dioscuri, whose Vedic counterparts appear as allies or consorts of the Dawn-goddess. I shall return to these issues in the chapters to follow.

Since I have left out data that seem less relevant to the main issues of the present study, this discussion has by no means been exhaustive as regards the whole repertoire of formulaic and onomastic parallels in early Indo-European texts. Further cases of scholarly progress should be mentioned if only to consolidate the sound basis of this procedure. Etymological equations that were for a long time considered fallacious, especially since they called to mind Friedrich Max Müller's and Adalbert Kuhn's Nineteenth century *Naturmythologie*, have been reconsidered by a new generation of linguists. Apart from using different and refined methods of comparison, these scholars have approached their subject matter from a new angle. Be-

---

[33] See, for instance, Boedeker (1974), Clader (1976), and Nagy (1990 [= 1978]).

[34] See discussion in Boedeker (1974: 24ff.) and Dunkel (1990: 9).

[35] Dunkel 1990: 10.

sides Dunkel's restored equation of the names *váruṇa* and οὐρανός, attention should be paid to Johanna Narten's suggestive notes on the etymology of the name of Prometheus (Doric Προμαθεύς), who is compared to Vedic Mātariśvan "robbing" (*mathnā́ti, √math* [sometimes with the preverb *pra-*]) the heavenly fire.[36] This new interpretation makes a strong case for the existence of an obsolete Greek compound name (derived from Indo-European **promāth₂eu̯-*) that was no longer semantically perceptible to the epic poets. Hesiod, for instance, associated the name with the verb μανθάνω. Michael Estell's reconsideration of the common background of Orpheus and R̥bhu (first suggested by Christian Lassen in 1840) is also noteworthy.[37] The names "Orpheus" and "R̥bhu" could indeed reflect the same underlying noun (**h₃r̥bhéu̯-*),[38] but Estell also adds that the two figures share similar verbal tags as regards their occupation (both are "craftsmen" associated with the verbal root *√*tetḱ*) and parentage (their fathers are "cudgel-bearers" associated with the noun **u̯aǵro-*).

As I hope to have shown in this short survey, the oral traditions providing the basis of poetic composition in the Archaic Age were themselves cast in a mould that preceded much of what we associate with the Hellenic tribes handing down these traditions. Some discrete comparisons may appear speculative or to be supported by accidental agreements, but if the body of evidence is considered as a whole there can be little doubt that certain aspects of Greek poetry (prosody, formulaics, divine epithets, etc.) formed a part of an Indo-European continuum, just as did the Greek dialects in which this poetry was expressed. The crucial issue is thus not the existence of such a continuum, but rather where it ends and to what extent it may

---

36 Narten 1960. Cf. Kuhn 1886: 18.

37 Estell 1999.

38 As I have pointed out elsewhere (Jackson 2002a: 84), there may be more to the meaning of this name than Estell himself considers.

still shed light upon the development of local phenomena? Before we touch upon these issues, however, it is advisable to invert the perspective and consider the development of early Greek poetry as forming a part of a Hellenic continuum.

## *The "Cyclic" Tradition*

The debate on the authorship, design, and transmission of the Homeric poems and the poems of the Epic Cycle has proceeded for at least two and a half millennia, making it one of the most tenacious scholarly debates in the West. It was a major concern of the Hellenistic philologists, but even the rhapsodes, who were the first to perform these poems, may have anticipated the editorial debate.[39] Since my own project does not directly relate to the final acquisition of epic poetry, but rather to that which preceded it, this section is only meant to serve as a background based on some recent scholarly achievements. In his new book *The Tradition of the Trojan War in Homer & the Epic Cycle*, Jonathan S. Burgess gives a thorough and updated survey of the early history of epic poetry in Greece. I shall follow his lead in trying to give a short summary of this topic.

References to the "Epic Cycle" in Greek literature usually concern a particular collection of epic poems, beginning with the union of Gaia and Uranus and closing with the return and death of Odysseus. Although titles of such poems have survived (*Titanomachy, Oedipodia, Thebais, Epigoni,* and those specifically concerning the Trojan War [the so called "Trojan Cycle"]: *Cypria, Aethiopis, Little Iliad, Iliou Persis, Nosti, Telegony*), the poems themselves can only be discerned through a small number of fragments and prose summaries. Alongside the Homeric poems, which at least in some

[39] Burgess 2001: 13.

sense were considered to belong to the Cycle (the *Iliad* following the *Cypria*, and the *Odyssey* following the *Nosti*), these and possibly other, no longer familiar epic poems constituted an indispensable narrative resource, from which the Archaic lyrical poets and the Attic tragedians collected their material.

The Epic Cycle was most likely manufactured in order to create a coherent collection of epic poetry during a period subsequent to the creation of the individual poems. Although the notion of a "cycle" of epic poetry may itself be very old,[40] the collection referred to as the "Epic Cycle" was evidently familiar to the authors of the Hellenistic period, but need not be much older than that.[41] Nevertheless, some of the poems used in the manufacturing of the Epic Cycle may at least belong to the Archaic Age, and the oral tradition on which these poems were based was in its turn much older. Burgess labels this tradition the "Cyclic" tradition, and his definition of this term will remain implicit throughout this study. By "Cyclic" tradition he means "the living pre-Homeric tradition of the Trojan War that led to the Trojan War poems in the Epic Cycle and continued with the Cycle as a major manifestation of it. This tradition preceded the Homeric poems but then in turn was gradually overshadowed by them."[42]

Despite the enormous influence of Homeric poetry on literature and visual art in the Classical and Hellenistic periods, it is evident

---

40 We have already seen that the metaphorical description of the craft of poetry as the joining together of a wheel or a chariot may belong to an Indo-European poetic heritage. This point is stressed by Gregory Nagy (1996: 89-91), who also links this metaphor to the name of Homer ("he who joins together" *homo-* + *ar-*), arguing that (p. 90) "if this etymology is correct, then the making of the Cycle, the sum total of epic, by the master Homer is a metaphor that pictures the crafting of the ultimate chariot-wheel by the ultimate carpenter or 'joiner.'"

41 Burgess 2001: 7ff.

42 Burgess 2001: 33.

that the tradition of the Trojan War was still an independent oral tradition in the Archaic Age. Whenever motifs outside the Homeric corpus appear to represent the same or similar scenes as those found in the *Iliad* or the *Odyssey*, we should consequently not take for granted that some of the Homeric poems had served as the main source of artistic inspiration. As a matter of fact, the majority of Trojan War images represented by artwork from the Eighth and Seventh century are not even found in (or are at least not in direct accord with) the Homeric poems, but should rather be defined as "Cyclic."[43] As regards the earliest Greek lyric, many scholars would still insist that phrases and similes attested in Homer can only recur in other (and younger) poetic texts as Homeric allusions. This idea is most likely wrong and is probably maintained due to the canonization of the Homeric poetry in later periods. In most cases, discoveries of "intertextuality" in the early lyric would rather point to the existence of a shared oral tradition (including formulas, phrases, and collocations of words) than to a submission to the supremacy of Homeric poetry.[44] It is also unlikely that the material found in the Epic Cycle merely reflects a post-Homeric ambition to fill in the gaps left by the Homeric poems. This ambition may well have characterized the compilation of the Cyclic material in the Hellenistic period, but the individual poems could still have sprung from the same Cyclic tradition as the Homeric poems. Since this was a fluid oral tradition, and since the poems were probably composed and transmitted orally long before they were written down, it would be misleading to imagine a fixed date of origin. But even if the poems of the Epic Cycle were composed in post-Homeric times (as most scholars assume), it does not necessarily follow that they were dependent on or inspired by the Homeric poems. Some of the problems traditionally associated with the so-called "Homeric Question" would thus rather

---

43 Burgess 2001: 53-114.

44 Burgess 2001: 114-131.

concern the development of the Cyclic tradition as a whole, not so much the creation of the Homeric poems as such. That this tradition reaches far back in prehistory is generally accepted, but is it possible to be more specific when it comes to characterizing its constituents and approximating its age?

A focal point of the Greek epic, the city of Troy or Ilios (*Ϝίλιος) has since the days of Heinrich Schliemann been identified with the ruins on the hill of Hisarlık on the eastern shores of the Dardanelles. With the discovery of Hittite and the other Anatolian languages, furthermore, the period and area to which the Trojan legends seem to refer slowly emerged from the darkness of prehistory. It is now generally assumed that the name and location of the city of Ilios coincides with that of the place referred to by the Hittites in the Second millenium BC as Wilusa. The "Cyclic" tradition is consequently not the only historical fact that has to be acknowledged here, but also parts of the narrative it transmitted.

Around 1290 BC, the kingdom and city of Wilusa was drawn into conflicts involving the prince Pijamaradu from the lands of Arzawa, the kings of the lands of Aḫḫijawa, and the great Hittite kingdom. Form the early Fourteenth century BC onwards, Mycenean culture had constituted an important element of power along the coast of Asia Minor, not least through its early presence in Milawanda (Miletus). There is little doubt that the people of Aḫḫijawa, as referred to in Hittite sources from the archives of Ḫattuša (the capitol of the great Hittite kingdom), should be identified with the Mycenean Greeks and the name Aḫḫijawa (or Aḫḫia) seen as an early reflex of the ethnonym 'Αχαιοί. In the second half of the Fourteenth century BC, the Hittite armies of Mursili II attacked Arzawa, which was at that time the most powerful state in western Asia Minor. This caused the king of Arzawa, Uḫḫaziti, to flee from his capitol Abasa (Ephesus), seeking the protection of the kings of Aḫḫiwava on the Greek mainland. Although Uḫḫaziti died soon after his exile, his family remained in the lands of Aḫḫiwava. The eagerness of this royal family to regain power in its native country was most likely an underlying reason for the prince Pijmaradu (probably the uncle of Uḫḫaziti) to begin political and military campaigns along the coastal districts of Asia Minor. In doing so he was supported by the kings of Aḫḫiawa, who allowed him to use Milawanda as a base of his campaigns. As an effect of these activities, Pijamaradu also posed a direct threat to the kingdom of Wilusa, which was provided with military support from the neighbouring state Sēḫa through instruction of the Hittite king. Since the Hittites were concerned about the political stability in western Asia Minor, and since King Alaksandus of Wilusa wanted to secure his position on the throne, Alaksandus concluded a treaty with the Hittite king Muwatilli II (1290-1272 BC), which turned Wilusa into a Hittite vassal state. In a letter (the so called Tawaglawa-letter) from the Hittite King Ḫattusili II (ca 1265-1240 BC), the king of Aḫḫiawa is urged to bring pressure to bear on Pijamaradu, with whom Ḫattusili wants to arrange a meeting. It remains unclear if these efforts paid off or not, nor do we know if Alaksandus still ruled in Wilusa at that time.[45]

The picture of the complex political history of western Asia Minor in the second half of the Second millenium BC is obviously rather blurred, and it almost invariably derives from Hittite sources. Still it is tempting to see in some of the names of cities, countries, peoples, and persons a pattern that is echoed in the Greek legends of the Trojan War. It would of course be wrong to approach the Trojan tradition as the representation of historical facts, but some of the events referred to in the Hittite sources may very well have triggered the shaping of the epic traditions passed on by the Greeks. The very few historical facts that can be distinguished in this elastic epic tradition seem to reappear in a heavily distorted form. The only attested

[45] For a comprehensive treatment of these issues, see Starke 1997.

kings of Wilusa are Alaksandus and his predecessor Kukkunni, but in Greek epic the name Kukkunni only (but not certainly) comes out as the name of a Trojan ally (Kyknos). The name Alaksandus undoubtedly matches Greek Alexandros, the other name of the Trojan prince Paris, but the name Priamos can at best be interpreted as a reflex of the Luvian name *Pari-muwas* (without any documented associations with Wilusa). It is significant that Alaksandus, in the treaty mentioned above, calls the gods of the city as his witnesses, among which the only god mentioned, Appaliunas (the possible restoration of *]a-ap-pa-li-u-na-aš* as preceded by a lost ideogram DINGIR denoting "god"), is closely reminiscent of Apollo (**apeli̯ōn*), the patron of Troy in the Greek epic.[46] The fact that Alaksandus bore a Greek name suggests that he had near relations to the people of Aḫḫijawa, but this people nevertheless posed an indirect threat to his kingdom by supporting Pijamaradu. It seems reasonable to assume that Anatolian languages were spoken in Wilusa at the time of Alaksandus (especially Luvian[47]), and the description of Trojan institutions in Greek epic (such as levirate marriage) occasionally correspond to Anatolian institutions.[48] There are, however, neither archaeological nor historical indications of a sack of Wilusa during the Mycenean period.

As we might expect, the discrepancy between documented history and epic memory is quite profound, yet nothing excludes that songs of (W)ilios were already beginning to appear in the Mycenean period,[49] or that these songs were to become a mainstay in the devel-

---

46 Cf. dicussion in Watkins 1994 (= 1986) and 1995: 149.

47 As Frank Starke points out, this is even suggested by the representation of the name "Wilusa" in Hittite sources.

48 Watkins 1994 (= 1986): 705f.

49 It is even possible that the Luvians performed epic songs about the city of Wilusa (a "Wilusiad"), although nothing can be said of their content. This was first suggested by Calvert Watkins (1994 (= 1986): 713ff.), who found a Luvian analogue to the expression ϝίλιος αἰπεινή ("steep Ilios"), the traditional Ho-

opment of the "Cyclic" tradition. Common media of such traditions were probably the hexameter and other hereditary techniques of oral composition, because there is nothing to suggest that written records were used by the Greeks for such purposes before the Eighth century BC. Even long after the development of alphabetic writing, the composition and performance of epic poetry remained a predominantly oral concern. Some metrical irregularities in early epic poetry can in fact be restored if the formulas are transformed into the language of the Pylos tablets or an even earlier stage of linguistic development, for which there is only comparative evidence. This and other circumstances, such as freedom in the placing of preverbs, have led many to believe that the tradition of epic song as we know it at least reaches back to the early Mycenean period (ca 1700 BC).[50]

Since there is both external and internal evidence for the use of metrical patterns and a poetic vocabulary that precede the historical period to which the epic poems seem to refer, it is reasonable to assume that this prehistoric period consisted of more than empty techniques and obsolete vocabulary. Many of the narratives were probably just as traditional as the narrative techniques. As suggested by the treatment of indigenous myths in Rome,[51] it is possible that the Greeks located myths in a historical or pseudo-historical environment. In the Archaic and Classical periods, however, the Mycenean past was already distant enough to become associated with a mythical past, and many of the persons and places associated with this age had already become the foci of religious attention. Consequently,

---

meric epithet for Troy, in the isolated Luvian verse (KBo 4.11,46) *aḫḫ=ata=ta alati awienta Wilušati* ("When they came from steep Wilusa"). The same epithet probably recurs in the fragmentary paragraph (KUB 35.102 (+) 103 iii 11) *ālati=tta aḫḫa LÚ-iš awita* [ ("When the the man came from steep [...]").

50 Joachim Latacz's discussion (with comprehensive bibliography) in Der neue Pauly, s.v. "Epos."

51 See especially Georges Dumézil 1966.

the stories located in this environment should not first of all be held accountable to a partly forgotten historical past, nor should we assume that they originally developed in this environment. As I intend to show in the follwoing chapters, important aspects of the thematic framework subsequently associated with the tradition of the Trojan War may respond to a much older, extra-Trojan tradition, which was perhaps more coherent than earlier assumed. It is accordingly not only the echoes of discrete mythical motifs in Greek epic that shall concern us in the following, but also their logic of combination.

The second part of this study is especially concerned with the emergence and characteristics of figures such as Zeus, Helen, and the Dioscuri, who trigger a series of epic events (e.g. the Trojan War and the wrath of Achilles), whereas the third part of this study is concerned with the way in which the conclusion of the series recalls its origin. This structure cannot be regarded as manifest in the extant Greek tradition, because the return and death of Odysseus no longer recalls the birth of Helen. Nevertheless, Homeric poetry still provides important clues to such a structure. In so far as a similar structure recurs in Vedic poetry, however, it is not in the form of an extensive epic narrative, but in the form of allusions to stories that all involve the same characters. A new story unfolds in the more or less overt biographical and genealogical facts.

# II.
# FATHER HEAVEN, HEAVEN'S DAUGHTER, AND THE DIVINE TWINS

The tradition of Helen and the Dioscuri exhibits some archaic features that have attracted much attention over the years, especially among scholars interested in the Indo-European aspects of Greek mythology. The issue has been dealt with in different methodological fashions. Furthermore, scholarly opinions diverge as to the general value and scope of Indo-European comparanda in the field of mythology. Although I principally remain optimistic to this endeavor, I would agree with some recent critics that such approaches could run the risk of producing contemporary myths instead of highlighting old ones.[52] I argued above that the notion of an Indo-European "culture" should be treated with particular caution, not because such a culture could never have existed, but because it seems futile to reconstruct such a complex and changeable quantity on the basis of what other cultures have passed on as parts of their own heritage.

This chapter is concerned with recurrent themes and onomastic traits in Greek mythology that seem to have the same (or a similar) background as the Vedic treatment of the Sky-god's (Dyaus) desire for his own daughter. Although the series of successive components are far from identical in the two traditions, their interference is unpredictable to such an extent that it seems reasonable to assume development from a shared tradition. I will start from descriptions of the conception and birth of Helen and the Dioscuri. Instead of moving immediately from this topic to that of the Vedic Dioscuri (the Aśvins or Nāsatyas), I continue by addressing some details in

---

[52] See especially Lincoln 1999.

the thematization of conception and birth as they recur elsewhere in Greek mythology. I then turn my attention to the figure of Dawn and some of the themes and figures with which she was associated in Greek mythology. The presentation of Vedic and post-Vedic comparanda highlights two narrative motifs (the rape of the Dawn-goddess and the wedding of Saraṇyū), and explains how these motifs can be linked together within the Vedic tradition. Additionally, I compare the Greek and the Vedic data in order to indentify possible hereditary traits.

## *The Rape of Nemesis*

The ancestry of Helen and the Dioscuri could be rendered quite differently in early Greek literature. This is apparent from the scholia to Pindar, *Nem.* 10,80: "Hesiod, however, may have rendered Helen (a child) neither of Leda nor of Nemesis, but of a daughter of Ocean and Zeus" (ὁ μέντοι Ἡσίοδος οὔτε Λήδας οὔτε Νεμεσέως δίδωσι τὴν Ἑλένην, ἀλλὰ θυγατρὸς Ὠκεανοῦ καὶ Διός). Both Leda and Nemesis could be regarded as mothers of all three children in two distinct (but similar) versions of the same tradition. The notion that Leda was the mother to the Dioscuri, but merely adopted the daughter of Nemesis (as suggested by Apollodorus [*Lib.* 3,10,7]), need not be more than an attempt to synthesize two contradictory versions. The possibility that Hesiod regarded Helen as a child, not of Nemesis or Leda, but of Zeus and an unspecified Oceanid, is particularly confusing in the light of the fact that Ocean was understood as the father of Nemesis according to some authors (e.g. Pausanias 7,5,3). If, on the other hand, Hesiod really did refer to a "'θυγατήρ Ὠκεανοῦ" as the mother of Helen, it is unlikely that he had Nemesis in mind. It is also unlikely that the scholiast failed to recognize Nemesis as the daughter of Ocean, because Hesiod explicitly asserts that

Nemesis was the daughter of Night (*Theog*. 223-24: τίκτε δὲ καὶ Νέμεσιν, πῆμα θνητοῖσι βροτοῖσι, / Νὺξ ὀλοή) who *had laid with no one* (*Theog*. 213: οὔ τινι κοιμηθεῖσα).

The story of Zeus and Nemesis in the *Cypria* is probably the earliest full treatment of the conception of Helen. The passage in all likelihood preceded a now lost treatment of the conception and birth of the Dioscuri. Although the text clearly indicates that the Dioscuri were conceived earlier (in contrast to some latter accounts of the story of Leda and the Swan), it is never explicitly stated that they had another mother. According to *Il*. 3,238, Helen had "the same" mother as the Dioscuri (τώ μοι μία γείνατο μήτηρ). There is to my knowledge no explicit reference to Leda as the mother of Helen in Homer, Hesiod, or the Epic Cycle (the earliest evidence is apparently Euripides *Hel*. 16-22, 257-9 and *Iph. Aul*. 49-51, 794-800), but according to the so-called *Nekyia*, Leda is the mother of the Dioscuri (*Od*. 11,298). An early reflex of the notion that Leda adopted someone else's offspring is Sappho (PMG. 166: "once Leda found a dark blue egg" [ποτα Λήδαν ὐακίνθινον [...] ὤιον εὔρεν]). This fragment could be an early testimony of the tradition referred to by Apollodorus, but it need not derive from exactly the same source as the *Cypria*. Although the *Cypria* does not seem to have contained the tradition that Helen and the Dioscuri were born from the same egg, such traditions may very well have existed.[53] The argument that this motif was borrowed from the tradition of Leda[54] is inconclusive, because both traditions (Leda and Nemesis giving birth to an egg after being raped by Zeus) are so strikingly similar that they are likely to have a common background. It seems reasonable to assume the different versions (Nemesis and Zeus as the parents of Helen or both Helen and the Dioscuri, Leda and Zeus as the parents of the Dioscuri and/or Helen, Leda and Zeus as the parents of Polydeuces and Helen, Leda adopting someone else's

---

53 E.g. the scholia to Lycophron 88 and to Callimachus, Dian. 232.

54 RE, s.v. "Nemesis" 2344.

offspring [Helen and/or the Dioscuri])[55] could all be old, but that none of them reveals the original identity of the mother. It seems unlikely, however, that both Leda and Nemeis occurred in one and the same version as victims of rape by Zeus in the form of a swan and then giving birth to one egg each, whereupon Leda finds and hatches the egg of Nemesis. The versions in which Leda functions as Helen's wet-nurse did probably not (at least not at an early date) contain the story of Leda and the swan. As suggested by a fragment of Philodemus' book Περὶ εὐσέβεια,[56] antique authors must have noticed that the two motifs (the metamorphosis and the birth of an egg) were strikingly similar. Having referred to the story of Nemesis as related in the *Cypria* (τὰ Κύ[πρια), Philodemus states that Zeus "in like manner" (ὥσ[π]ε[ρ) transformed himself into a swan when he desired Leda. This observation clearly indicates that Philodemus was familiar with what happened to be (although he may not have been aware of it himself) alternative versions of the same tradition, not with discrete motifs in unconnected traditions or successive motifs in the same version of this tradition.

The passage in the *Cypria* reads as follows:

τοὺς δὲ μέτα τριτάτην Ἑλένην τέκε, θαῦμα βροτοῖσι
[---][57]
τήν ποτε καλλίκομος Νέμεσις φιλότητι μιγεῖσα

---

55 RE, s.v. "Leda," 1119f.

56 Wilhelm Crönert 1901: 109.

57 Friedrich Gottlieb Welcker (1849: 514) was the first scholar to suggest that Athenaeus may have left out some verses from the *Cypria* between the first and the second verse of the quotation. Athenaeus cited the *Cypria* because he wanted to show that its author represented Nemesis changing into a fish, and the first line would then clarify who was intended by τὴν in the second line. To Welcker, as I understand his argumentation, a lacuna would make it more probable that Nemesis was the subject of τέκε in the first line, which also seems to have been the opinion of Athenaeus. It is not entirely clear, however, if the tradition of emending the text with a lacuna between Line 1 and 2 (as passed on

Ζηνὶ θεῶν βασιλῆι τέκεν κρατερῆς ὑπ᾽ ἀνάγκης.
φεῦγε γὰρ οὐδ᾽ ἔθελεν μιχθήμεναι ἐν φιλότητι
πατρὶ Διὶ Κρονίωνι· ἐτείρετο γὰρ φρένας αἰδοῖ
καὶ νεμέσει· κατὰ γῆν δὲ καὶ ἀτρύγετον μέλαν ὕδωρ
φεῦγεν, Ζεὺς δ᾽ ἐδίωκε· λαβεῖν δ᾽ ἐλιαίετο θυμῶι.
ἄλλοτε μὲν κατὰ κῦμα πολυφλοίσβοιο θαλάσσης
ἰχθύι εἰδομένη, πόντον πολὺν ἐξορόθυνεν,
ἄλλοτ᾽ ἀν᾽ Ὠκεανὸν ποταμὸν καὶ πείρατα γαίης,
ἄλλοτ᾽ ἀν᾽ ἤπειρον πολυβώλακα· γίγνετο δ᾽ αἰεὶ
θηρί᾽ ὅσ᾽ ἤπειρος αἰνὰ τρέφει, ὄφρα φύγοι νιν.
(Fr. 7, Davies)

"Third after them she (he?) gave birth to Helen, a wonder to mortals [...]; whom lovely-haired Nemesis bore, united in love to Zeus the king of the gods, under harsh compulsion. For she ran away, not wanting to unite in love with father Zeus the son of Kronos, tormented by inhibition and misgiving: across land and dark, barren water she ran, and Zeus pursued, eager to catch her; sometimes in the noisy sea's wave, where she had the form of a fish, as he stirred up the mighty deep; sometimes along Ocean's stream and the ends of the earth; sometimes on the loam-rich land; and she kept changing into all the fearsome creatures that the land nurtures, so as to escape him." (Tr. Martin West)

Although the impending rape may certainly be a sufficient cause for Nemesis' shame and anger, it seems as if Hugh G. Evelyn-White, in his translation of the passage ("*her* father"), took πατήρ in Line 5 as implying more than a casual usage of the epithet "father Zeus." Such an assumption would fit well into the general pattern discussed towards the end of this chapter, but the recognition of hints about incest in this or other texts dealing with the conception of Helen and the Dioscuri should not be based on wishful thinking. Even though Nemesis was referred to as "Διὸς παῖς" under the name of "Adrasteia" (Euripides,

---

in the editions of Bethe, Allen, and Davies) has been maintained for the reason originally proposed by Welcker.

*Rhes.* 342),[58] it would seem far-fetched to regard incest as a leading topic in the passage quoted from the *Cypria*. Furthermore, the paternal genealogy of Nemesis is rather ambiguous.[59] The link between Nemesis and Adrasteia remains interesting for another reason, because the later men of Troy are told to have worshiped the apotheosized Helen as "Adrasteia."[60] This identification perfectly balances Helen's association with the word νέμεσις (literally meaning "retribution" or, more specifically, "righteous anger") in the *Iliad*, or the attribution of the word πῆμα ("misery") to both figures (Nemesis [e.g. *Theog.* 592] and Helen [e.g. *Il.* 3,50-51]) in epic poetry.[61] Another indication of a confluence in the cult of the two figures is the characterization of Helen as "Rhamnousian" in Callimachus (*Hymn to Artemis* 232), which echoes the cult of Nemesis at Rhamnous in Attica.[62] In their mutual roles as instruments or manifestations of divine retribution, Nemesis and Helen were probably not genealogically associated before the emergence of the Cyclic tradition, and it is therefore plausible that such epic reinterpretations were preceded by traditions that had a different shape as regards the identity of mother and daughter. This assumption could partly explain inconsistencies in the epic and post-epic renderings of Helen's parentage.

A story told by Pausanias in his *Description of Greece* (2,22,6) supports the idea that certain patterns in the stories of Nemesis/Leda recurred in the story of Helen's adolescence. He says that she became pregnant as a captive of Theseus, who had snatched her from

---

58 The Attic tragedians evidently used "Adrasteia" as an epithet of Nemesis (cf. also Aeschylus, *Prom.* 935: οἱ προσκυνοῦντες τὴν 'Αδράστειαν σοφοί "those who do obeisance to Adrasteia (lit. 'that-which–cannot-be-run-away-from') are wise" (J. E. Harry 1905: 292). Cf. the expression προσκυνῶ δὲ τὴν Νέμεσιν at the end of a letter (Alciphron, Ep. 1,33).

59 H. Herter 1935 (RE XVI 2, 2362).

60 Farnell 1921: 324 and Welcker 1849: 135

61 See discussion in Austin 1994: 43.

62 Austin 1994: 43.

the dancing-ground (a motif to which we shall return briefly below). While Theseus had gone with Pirithous to Thesprotia, Helen secretly gave birth to Iphigenia in Argos. Having founded the sanctuary of Eileithya at the place of Iphigenia'a birth, she gave her baby to Clytemnestra.

The stories of Nemesis and Leda are certainly not the only ones in Greek mythology involving what could be loosely defined as "bestial rape."[63] By approaching such stories from a sociological perspective, J. E. Robson understands them as being didactic and symbolic treatments of the attitudes towards marriageable females' views of marriage and male sexuality, which helped defining and upholding the institutions of the Greek city-state and the Greek world-order.[64] They were focused on the boundaries that should not be crossed by women in order to avoid rape, but also on the dangers of resisting sanctioned sex. According to Robson, the "bestial" myth usually takes on one of three typical forms: 1) The god is transformed into an animal and rapes the girl (Antiope/Zeus, Canace/Poseidon, Dryope/Apollo, Europa/Zeus, Leda/Zeus, Melantho/Poseidon, Persephone/Zeus, Philyra/Kronos). 2) The girl is transformed into an animal but is nevertheless raped (Metis/Zeus, Psamathe/Aeacus, Taygete/Zeus, Thetis/Peleus). 3) Both god and girl are changed into an animal before the sexual act (Asterie/Zeus [or Poseidon], Nemesis/Zeus, Theophane/Poseidon).[65] As exemplified by the stories of Nemesis and Leda, however, alternative versions of the same tradition need not be restricted to the same group. Although "rape" is used as a keyword by Robson, caution should be observed insofar as the word is considered to exclude subsequent consent to sex. The rape of women in Greek mythology may in fact often, especially if the perpetrator is a god, be classified as

---

63 For a discussion of this topic, see Robson 1997: 65-96.

64 Robson 1997: 82f.

65 Robson 1997: 74.

seduction rather than rape, because several accounts of such encounters neither speak of disgrace nor of forcible abduction.[66]

Further attention to the sociological subtext of this theme may proceed from the observation that bestial rape or seduction often results in heroic offspring. There is also, and more specifically, a set of stories in which Zeus or Poseidon beget twins that are subsequently recognized as progenitors or founders of cities. Some of these are listed in the *Nekyia* (Neleus and Pelias from Poseidon and Tyro [11,235ff.], Amphion and Zethus from Zeus and Antiope [11,260ff.]), others occur elsewhere but nevertheless convey an archaic impression (Aeolos and Boeotos from Poseidon and Melanippe, Minos and Rhadamanthys [and Sarpedon] from Zeus and Europa). The typical scheme manifests itself variously: 1) Zeus or Poseidon, when desiring a goddess or woman, have a habit of shifting shape (sometimes in order to conceal their identity). 2) The object of desire may change her shape in order to escape her pursuer. 3) She is likely to give birth to a human child or a pair of twins. 4) She is forced to hide her offspring or to abandon it, whereupon it is found and nurtured by someone else (preferably an animal and eventually, a shepherd). 5) The offspring will be distinguished as heroic, as progenitor of a people, or as founder of a city.

The story of Poseidon and Melanippe is particularly interesting in the light of the Vedic data to be considered. One of the different versions (*Diod.* 4,67,2) suggests that Poseidon (as Hippote) transformed himself insto a horse and raped Melanippe. A similar hippomorphic trait is seen in the name Melanippe (meaning "black mare"). Melanippe gives birth to twins (Aeolos and Boeotos), but is blinded and locked up in a shelter by her father while the twins are abandoned in the wilderness. The twins are nurtured by a cow, brought up by

66 Lefkowiz 1993.

shepherds, and eventually become progenitors of the Aeolians and Boeotians (e.g. Hygin's *Fabulae* 186).

It is easy to recognize in such stories typical markers of kingship and authorizations of power. The first ruler is descended from a god, he is left behind by his real parents, and eventually turns up among humans (often through the medium of a shepherd) beyond the locus of conception and birth, as if fallen from the sky, without any predecessors that would otherwise have obstructed the image of a primordial and incompatible ruler. The *Nekyia* also alludes to the story of Leda and the Dioscuri (11,298ff.), suggesting that the Dioscuri (although here regarded as the sons of Tyndareus) conformed to the same aetiological pattern. This assumption is in fact supported by a passage in Herodotus (5,75), according to whom the Dioscuri played an important role in the dynastic legends of Sparta. It is noteworthy that the divine nature of the Dioscuri is not taken for granted in the *Nekyia*, but that they rather appear as apotheosized heroes. Whenever similarities of this kind are adduced as signs of a common heritage, however, it should be kept in mind that recurrent features in such dynastic legends (descent from animals, abandonment of children in the wilderness, the cult of twins) are well attested in societies outside the framework of any conceivable genetic connections. A useful description of the genre from a typological perspective is found in Gerhard Binder's 1961 Erlangen dissertation *Die Aussetzung des Königkindes Kyros und Romulus.*

The next step in this investigation is to consider themes and figures that were not directly (or by necessity) associated with bestial rape, but with a more complex structure in which metamorphosis and rape could form integrated parts. By looking closer at such themes, it is my hope that earlier and less transparent traditions may be uncovered. An important issue in this connection is the dancing-ground (or χορός), which seems to have constituted a typical locus of sexual arousal and rape in early Greek literature.

A key event in the Cyclic tradition, the mating of Zeus and Nemesis is comparable with that of Peleus and Thetis in many respects. First of all, the two stories contain similar thematic traits, especially as regards the function of shape-shifting. Secondly, the progenies resulting from two events, Helen and Achilles, have further characteristics in common with regard to their roles in the epic plot. Both figures are causes for the war and subsequent sufferings around which the whole tradition revolves, they are a πῆμα ("misery") for mankind. In this role, the two figures constitute essential parts in the fulfillment of Zeus' plan to relieve the Earth of overpopulation (cf. *Cypria*, Fr. 1, Davies).[67] The interpretation of Helen and Achilles as the instruments of the Διὸς βουλή is salient in the scholiastic tradition, and it is conceivable that a story of over- and depopulation was the source from which the Cyclic tradition developed in the first place.[68] Another common feature of Helen and Achilles emerges from the fact that they are the only figures in the *Iliad* who desire their own deaths.[69] In the light of these facts, it is possible to consider the mythical rendering of Nemesis and Thetis as an appendage to the structural agreement of Helen and Achilles.

The story of Peleus and Thetis is hinted at by the epic poets, yet the shape-shifting motif is first attested with certainty in Pindar and the Tragedians. The motif is also seen on three Etruscan bronze tripods from around 520 BC.[70] Glenn W. Most's attempt to interpret Alcman's enigmatic cosmogonic fragment (Fr. 5, PMG) as an allusion to the story of Thetis' metamorphoses at least makes plausible the point that the story was already familiar in Seventh century

67 Mayer 1996: 12.

68 Mayer 1996: 1ff.

69 Mayer 1996: 12.

70 Krieger 1975: 10

Sparta.[71] As the story is told by Pindar and by others following his example, Zeus and Poseidon, both desiring the Nereid Thetis, are warned by Themis that the son of Thetis will be more powerful than his father. It is decided that Thetis is to be given as wife to the mortal Peleus. Peleus steals upon Thetis on a full moon evening, but in order to win her he has to hold her fast as she assumes different forms (fire, snake, lion, etc.). According to a papyrus from Herculaneum (Fr 2, Davies), both Hesiod and the author of the *Cypria* handed down a slightly different version of the story, in which Zeus swears that Thetis, in order to please Hera, has to become the wife of a mortal since she has avoided marriage with him.

Some scholars have drawn the conclusion that Thetis and the other Nereids were performing a ring-dance at the event of the rape.[72] This assumption certainly applies to the general literary and artistic characterization of the Nereids, but is to the best of my knowledge not backed up by any textual sources containing the story of Thetis' abduction. Nevertheless, variants of this tradition echoed in other stories, or supported by other media, seem to have localized Thetis and the other Nereids in a sacred dancing-ground (χορός) at the event of the rape. The Nereids are often depicted as dancers, not least at the wedding of Peleus and Thetis (cf. Euripides, *Ion* 1078ff., *Iph. Taur.* 427ff., *Iph. Aul.* 1055, Himerius [*Eclogue* XIII, 21]). In most of these passages the keyword is either the verb χορέω or the noun χορός. Dancing may also be hinted at in Alcman's fragment as interpreted by Most, especially with regard to an expression (μαρμαρυγάς) taken as a reference to the flashing of choral dancers' feet.[73] More important, however, are certain visual representa-

71 Most 1987.

72 Cf, for instance, M. Meyer (1937) (RE VI A, 209): "in einer Vollmondnacht, wie sie (Thetis) mit ihren Schwester-Nereiden den Reigen tanzt, lauert er (Peleus) ihr auf, springt hervor, um sie zu ergreifen."

73 Most 1987: 15f.

tions of Peleus and Thetis. The depictions on a Corinthian *Amphora a colonette* and a vase from Ruvo, first compared in an article by Botho Graef (1886), clearly indicate that Thetis was considered to be involved in a ring-dance with her sisters when Peleus (the amphora is also labeled with his name) stole upon her behind a tree.[74] Furthermore, the assumption that the place depicted on the Corinthian amphora had a cultic significance[75] is commensurate with the characterization of a traditional dancing-ground (or χορός) in early Greek literature (see below). Herodotus (7,191) mentions the coast of Sepias (Magnesia) as the place from which the Ionians thought that Thetis was carried off by Peleus. The place was said to belong to the Nereids and is referred to by Herodotus as a χῶρος (ὡς ἐκ τοῦ χώρου τούτου ἁρπασθείη ὑπὸ Πηλέος), a term that shares several conceptual associations with χορός and, as cautiously suggested by Pierre Chantraine,[76] may belong to the same family.[77]

In her study of the origins of Aphrodite, Deborah D. Boedeker regards the terms χορός and χῶρος as clues to the process through which this goddess entered into the Greek poetic tradition as a hypostasis of the Indo-European Dawn-goddess.[78] By proceeding from the observation that Aphrodite frequently occurs in the context of dance and song, especially with regard to formulas including the word χορός, Boedeker uses etymological and philological evidence to demonstrate that this term was associated with the abode of the Sun and Dawn. Among the several instances discussed in her book,

---

74 "Sicher dargestellt ist also ein Jüngling, den sich der Vasenmaler wohl (trotz ihrer Kleinheit) hinter einer Palme versteckt dachte, wie er einem Mädchen, das mit anderen einen Reigen tanzt, auflauert, um es zu fangen, und wahrscheinlich auf seinem gespann zu entführen." (Graef 1886: 194)

75 Cf. Krieger 1975: 14.

76 1968: 12.

77 Cf. the treatment of χορός and χῶρος in Boedeker's (1974) appendix, pp. 85-91.

78 Boedeker 1974: 43-63 and 85-91.

a particularly striking case is the reference to the abodes and dancing-grounds (οἰκία καὶ χοροί) of Eos at the island of Aiaia (*Od.* 12,1-4). Boedeker also shows that the word χορός sometimes refers to a dancing-ground that functioned as a type of cult place inherited from pre-Greek and archaic Greek religion. This cult was probably aimed at goddesses of fertility and growth, which in Greek society needed not be of chthonic origin. A less convincing argument for the solar and matutinal context of the term χορός is the reference to an underlying verbal root with the trivial semantic sense "to place, set" (√**ǵher*), which occasionally and not very surprisingly occurs in solar contexts. The Vedic Dawn-goddess can be shown to gravitate towards the same nexus of concepts as the one suggested by the term χορός in Greek, but despite the lack of an exact equivalent to this term in Vedic, such a nexus of concepts may still conform to the common background of Eos and Uṣas.

It is noteworthy that the dancing-ground was conceived as a typical site for a rape, both in epic accounts, in local myths, and in the quasi-historical story of the rape of the Spartan maidens as told by Pausanias (4,16,9).[79] Interesting in this connection are the accounts of Aphrodite (*H. Aph.* 117-118) and Helen (Plutarch, *Theseus* 31,2) being snatched up (ἀναιρέω) or abducted (αἱρέω) from the χορός while dancing as maidens in the honor of Artemis.[80] Another noteworthy aspect of Helen's abduction (this time by Paris) is hinted at in a late work by Photius (with references to a work by Ptolemy [*Hist. Nov.*]). He writes that some authors say that Helen was abducted (ἁρπασθῆναι) by Alexander/Paris while she, struck by his

79 Boedeker 1974: 48. Cf. also Lawler 1964: 42-43.

80 Further evidence of this kind (e.g. Plutarch *Parallela Minora* 40: Ἴδας [...] ἁρπάσας ἐκ χοροῦ) clearly shows that αἱρέω often collocates with the noun χορός. Cf. also Nagy's discussion of the verb αἱρέω in similar contexts (1990 [1973]: 242ff.).

beauty, followed him "like a god" (ὡς θεῷ).[81] It thus seems as if the pattern observed in stories about divine desire and rape was occasionally applied to the story of Helen and Paris. Furthermore, it seems as if Helen has equal status as Eos/Aphrodite and their relation to the χορός in a passage (*Il.* 3,391-394) interpreted by Boedeker as a simile:

> A passage in the *Iliad* may preserve a latent example of χορός used as home of a Dawn-goddess, in this case specifically Aphrodite. Having rescued Paris from his single combat with Menelaus, Aphrodite takes him to his chamber and goes to fetch Helen. She describes Paris' beauty to Helen, comparing him to a man just going to, or coming from the χορός:
>
> κεῖνος ὅ γ' ἐν θαλάμῳ καὶ δινωτοῖσι λέχεσσι,
> κάλλεΐ τε στίλβων καὶ εἵμασιν· οὐδέ κε φαίης
> ἀνδρὶ μαχεσσάμενον τόν γ' ἐλθεῖν, ἀλλὰ χορόνδε
> ἔρχεσθ', ἠὲ χοροῖο νέον λήγοντα καθίζειν.
>
> Several parallels may be drawn between this passage and others which deal with the Dawn and her lover. Paris is here distinguished by the remarkable beauty which also characterizes Eos' lovers Cleitus (ο 251-252) and Tithonus (*H. Aph.* 200-201, 218-219). Aphrodite returns him to his θάλαμος ["chamber"] as Eos brings Tithonus to her own θάλαμος (*H. Aph.* 235). She compares him to a man going to a χορός, and Eos home in the *Odyssey* has χοροί (μ 4). θάλαμος and χορός may be traditional elements preserved from more archaic versions of the story, in which both terms might have referred to the home of the Dawn goddess, where she keeps her mortal lover. Moreover, Helen's rebuke to Aphrodite a few lines [408-409] later overtly suggests that the Dawn-goddess herself is Paris' lover [---]. All these resemblances indicate that the myth of the Dawn-goddess and her lover may underlie some of the narrative patterns in the Aphrodite-Paris episode.[82]

We shall briefly touch upon antoher role of Thetis and her position within the thematic framework of the χορός. Not only is Thetis as-

---

[81] *Bilbliotheca*, 149a.

[82] Boedeker 1974: 61f.

sociated with the dancing-ground (as seen above) when subjected to rape, but in the *Iliad* (and other poems of the Epic Cycle, such as the *Aethiopis*) she also enters into a structurally homologous relationship with Eos. Both goddesses unite with mortal lovers (Peleus and Tithonos) and give birth to heroic sons (Achilles and Memnon). The two mothers are juxtaposed and mirrored in their roles as immortal guardians of the two heroes, and they even share some dictional features.[83] We noticed above that the homologous rendering of Helen and Achilles as instruments of divine retribution meets with a structural response in the mythical rendering of Nemesis and Thetis as their mothers, and so does the structural relationship between Thetis and Eos balance that of Achilles and Memnon. This narrative juxtaposition is also apparent in the visual arts.[84] Some may confine themselves to regarding such connections as synchronically significant,[85] but this does not imply that they are diachronically insignificant. Although it must be wrong to assume that structurally equivalent figures in the Cyclic tradition always developed from one and the same prototype, we might still expect instances of such repetitions to be the outcome of an evolutionary process. As long as the homologies within one and the same tradition are considered to be interdependent and not purely accidental, it should also be assumed that different properties of tradition have interfered over time in order for these homologies to develop, or that they emerged from a property unknown to us.

The figures and stories presented in this part of the chapter seem directly or indirectly associated with the dancing-ground as a locus of sexual arousal and rape. Apart from the links between Greek and

---

83 See discussion in Slatkin 1991: 21-33.

84 I refer to the popular depiction of the two heroes in single combat, their divine (sometimes winged) mothers standing behind them. Cf. LIMC, s.v. Achilleus XXV.

85 Cf. Slatkin 19991: 30-31.

Vedic data as regards the Greek Dawn-goddess and her χορός, another possible link between the two traditions in this regard is the often neglected fact that the Vedic Dawn-goddess is the object of rape in the context of theriomorphic transformation (a motif to be discussed in more detail below). We may thus cautiously argue that the χορός and its association with Eos constitutes an echo of such traditions in Greek myth, that these traditions were otherwise lost or transformed (sometimes almost beyond recognition) as they became the foci of epic song in the Cyclic tradition, and that the only way to retrieve their earlier features is to look for them in societies preserving different aspects of the same narrative heritage.

## *The Spartan Dawn*

The meaning of the term χορός was still ambiguous in the epic language. It could either refer to a place (a dancing-ground) or an activity (a ring-dance), and only occasionally is the intended sense of the term easily determinable (at *Od.* 8, 260 it almost certainly means "dancing-place," whereas "ring-dance" must be the intended sense at *Il.* 3,394). During later periods, the term was to an ever increasing extent applied to a "group of dancers and singers" (often young girls and/or boys).[86] It is this group of dancers that shall concern us here, especially the παρθένοι, or "maidens," in the Spartan choral performances.

With the exception of some meagre (possibly spurious) remains, Alcman provides the earliest (Seventh century) examples of Greek choral lyric poetry. The most extensive fragment, the Louvre Partheneion (PMG, 1) was composed for a chorus of Spartan girls led by two competing figures, called Hagesikhora and Agido. It seems as if

---

86 An early attestation is found in the *Shield of Herakles* 275-277.

Hagesikhora (who is explicitly referred to as χοραγός [Attic χορηγός] "chorus-leader") and Agido had special responsibilities in the course of the choral performance, such as looking after the chorus or conducting rites while the other girls were singing. Both are praised for their beauty and likened to running horses, perhaps a reference to an actual race or contest that took place as a part of the rite itself. Scholarly approaches to the overall meaning of the ritual have not yielded compatible results. The disagreement is particularly noticeable as regards the nature of the contest and the identity of the goddess (or goddesses) worshiped by the chorus as Orthria/Aotis. While reaching partly different conclusions, some scholars (Bowra, Calame, and Nagy) have argued for a link between the choral singers and/or Hagesichora/Agido and a guild of Spartan priestesses known as the Leukippides. The same scholars have also recognized a possible link between Helen and the enigmatic divinity Aotis (dative 'Αώτι[87] [85]). The priestly Leukippides, probably two in number and referred to as παρθένοι "maidens," were important figures in the Spartan cult of the mythical Leukippides (Hilaeira and Phoibe, consorts of the Dioscuri) and Dionysos.[88] Helen is said to join with the Leukippides in their dances (Euripides, *Helen* 1465-1466). In the song of the Spartan women at the end of Aritsophanes' *Lysistrata* (1308-15) she is described as the chorus-leader of a group of young girls who dance "like fillies" (χᾆτε πῶλοι). Πῶλοι is attested elsewhere as an epithet of the two Leukippides (Hesychius, s.v. πωλία).

Nagy stresses the mimetic aspects of the whole performance in Alcman's *Partheneion*, introducing typological (Navajo) comparanda to support this interpretation.[89] A similar tendency is found

87 The expected dative ending would be -τιδι, but the occasional dropping of δ and contraction of the two ι:s (resulting in a long -ī) is attested elsewhere (e.g. Doric Λιμνάτι), cf. Jurenka 1896: 29.

88 Calame 1977: 323ff.

89 Nagy 1996: 89f.

in Calame, who identifies the chorus-leader Hagesikhora with the goddess Aotis (= Helen). In doing so, he points to external Greek evidence regarding processes of identification and incarnation in the relation between the deity to whom a certain rite is devoted and the persons performing the rite. The basic reason for assuming Helen and the Leukippides to be implicitly present in Alcman's poem, however, is already given in Bowra.[90] He saw the Leukippides "as possible candidates for Alcman's Choir"[91] and cautiously argued for implicit references to Helen and her votaries in Alcman's description of the chorus, the chorus-leaders, and the goddess Aotis. Although he did not call particular attention to the formation and semantic sense of the name Aotis, he took it to be linguistically and in some sense pragmatically connected with Dor. Ἀώς. Page[92] accepted the linguistic association with the Doric word for "Dawn," but understood the appellative Aotis in the local sense "at the Dawn" (in a transferred sense "[living] in the East"), which he took as a pretext for the argument that Aotis was just another Laconian appelative of Artemis Orthia,[93] whose temple was situated to the east of the town of Sparta.[94] The sense of the denominative suffix -τις (masculine -της) should probably not be so strictly defined ("[t]he analogy [of Laconian apellatives of Artemis] suggests (or even demands) that

90 1960 [1st edition 1936].

91 Bowra 1960: 54.

92 1951: 74.

93 Page (1951: 71ff.) follows the scholiast, who reads Ὀρθίαι instead of ὀρθρίαι (Verse 61). Counter-arguments (inter alia on the basis of metrics) are found in Calame (1977: 119ff.).

94 Page does not discuss the Hellenistic compound προσηῴα, which was an epiclesis of Artemis in Euboea "from the position of her temple" (LSJ, s.v.) "towards the East." Although this could have supported his general assumption, it sheds no light upon the specific sense of Aotis.

'Αώτις be understood in a local sense" [p. 74]).[95] A less unyielding approach to the name as that of a "Dawn-goddess" (also suggested by the meaning of the epithet Orthria [cf. ὄρθριος "at daybreak, in the morning, early"]) was resumed by Antonio Garzya (1954) and Claude Calame (1977a). Garzya and Calame also adopted Bowra's idea that Aotis was a possible epiclesis of Helen (in the sense that she could be similar or identical with Eos/Aos).

Bowra adduced additional clues from his assumption. Most important among these is a passage in Theocritus' *Epithalamium for Helen* (18,26-28). Since Theocritus may have drawn the subject-matter of his poem from the now lost first book of Stesichorus' *Helen* (Argum. Theocr. 18), certain themes in the *Epithalamium* may indeed belong to an early choral tradition. Sung by Spartan maidens to honor Helen at her wedding, this "bridal song" (ὑμέναιος [8]) contains aspects of Helen that seem more rooted in local tradition than in pan-Hellenic epic themes. One such local tradition is the winding of a wreath of flowers growing close to the δρόμος at Sparta (38-48). The wreath is hung on a plane tree, under which oil is sprinkled, and the bark of the plane tree is inscribed with the words "I am Helen's plane tree" (Ἑλενας φυτόν εἰμι). The maidens (παρθενικαί [2]) dance and sing outside the bridal chamber (2-3), and while praising her beauty they evoke the name and attributes of Dawn:

> 'Αὼς ἀντέλλοισα καλὸν διέφανε πρόσωπον,
> πότνια Νύξ, τό λευκὸν ἔαρ χειμῶνος ἀνέντος·
> ὧδε καὶ ἁ χρυσέα Ἑλένα διεφαίνετ' ἐν ἁμῖν.

"Beautiful, Lady Night, is the face that rising Dawn reveals, or the bright spring when winter is over; and so among us did golden Helen shine." (Bowra [tr])

---

[95] Cf. Garzya 1954: 65f. (with reference to the examples of denominatives with the suffix -της listed in Debrunner 1917: §354).

Bowra by no means took this simile as evidence for a cult of Helen as Aotis, but he was still inclined to regard Helen as a better candidate for this epiclesis than the often suggested Artemis. Although likewise a patron of maidens in Sparta, Artemis is never demonstrably connected to or identified with Dawn.[96] He also points to the reference in Hesychius to a group of gods, "transported from the δρόμος to Samothrace and Lemnos," called the Ἄωοι, as a possible reference to a group of Spartan gods, including Helen and the Dioscuri, all of whom had their shrines near the δρόμος. Bowra speculates that the Doric title Ἄωοι "may have been connected with Helen's title of Ἀώτις." In support of this hypothesis, I would like to refer to the story of the Dioscuri and the sons of Hippocoön in the beginning of the *Partheneion*, claiming cautiously that there might be a link.

As mentioned above, the function of Helen and her festival (the Ἑλένεια) in Sparta seem to have had little to do with Homer's Helen. It is also significant that Isocrates (*Laud. Helenae* 63) writes that the Spartans offer to Helen and Menelaus in Therapnai "not as to heroes, but as to gods" (οὐχ ὡς ἥρωσιν ἀλλ' ὡς θεοῖς). There has been a tendency to describe the role of Helen in the Laconian cult in vague terms as a "fertility goddess." Others have pointed to the fact that some of the votive gifts found in her temple in Therapnai resemble those found at the sanctuary of Artemis Orthia.[97] More substantial information about Helen's cult in Sparta comes from litereary sources mentioning the important role of adolescent girls. During her festival, the Ἑλένεια, the maidens of Sparta were carried to Helen's temple in wicker carriages, so called κάνναθρα.[98]

---

96 Cf. Bowra 1960: 52.

97 As regards Helen and Artemis Orthia, see also above. For a short discussion of the archeological findings from the Menelaion in Therapnai, see Deoudi 1999: 124f. Clader (1976: 69, 74f.) considers further prallels in the Laconian cults of Helen and Artemis Orthia.

98 Clader 1976: 68.

Another discrepancy regarding the reception of Helen in Sparta is the rendering of her name with initial digamma.[99] Although this form was evidently in use during the Sixth century, there is also early evidence for writing the name without initial digamma in dialects (such as the Doric dialect of Corinth) where this letter was retained and where the inclination to render the names of gods and heroes according to epic conventions appears to have been less pronounced. Consequently, we should take into account the possibility that two names of diffrerent origin were occasionally subjected to merger in the treatment of the figure known as "Helen" in the Spartan context. This issue, which is of crucial importance to the etymological interpretation of the name, will be further considered below.

Before closing this discussion of Helen as a possible hypostasis of Eos, especially in a Laconian context, some further clues should be taken into consideration. It has been suggested elsewhere that the Homeric epithets Διὸς θυγάτηρ/θυγάτηρ Διός "daughter of Zeus," the exact formal cognates of which (*divá[s] duhitár-/duhitár- divás* "daughter of Dyaus") invariably apply to Uṣas in the Vedic hymns, are particularly assigned to Greek goddesses that fulfill diffrerent inherited functions of Eos.[100] The fact that Eos herself is never called Διὸς θυγάτηρ/θυγάτηρ Διός in Homer cannot be explained on the sole basis of divergent traditions regarding her descent (such as *Theog.* 371-47: Hyperion), but may in fact also, as demonstrated by Gregory Nagy, have had metrical reasons.[101] Helen is only called Διὸς θυγάτηρ once in Homer (*Od.* 4,227). It has been suggested that the quality of Helen's behaviour in this scene (where she is acting both as beneficient and malevolent lady) is signalled by the epithet.[102] While there is not, I submit, enough evidence in Homer for

---

[99] Catlin/Cavanagh 1976.

[100] Nagy 1979:200. See also Boedeker 1974, especially pp. 18-42.

[101] Nagy 1990 [1973]: 247f.

[102] Clader 1976: 53.

stressing a general conformity between Helen and Eos, the passage could still be treated as a clue. An interesting discrepancy in the Homeric usage of the epithet Διὸς θυγάτηρ is touched upon by Clader. She points out that Helen is the only "mortal" among other ladies in the Epic who is called a child of Zeus, and that "in an Indo-European context it stands to reason that if Zeus is going to take the trouble to beget a mortal, he will get a son."[103] In other words, Helen does not unambiguously belong to the heroic plane from the point of view of Homeric diction.

A last, albeit rather weak link between Helen and Eos can be established on the basis of iconographic evidence. On an Etruscan mirror from the Borgia collection (Gerhard 1840, plate CXCVI), for instance, a crowned goddess with a team of four horses (typical features of Θesan, the Etruscan equivalent of Eos/Aurora) is depicted in the background of Helen and her suitors. Calame draws attention to this particular mirror and other Etruscan depictions, arguing that they complete the otherwise meagre visual and literary references that associate the figures of Helen and Eos.

A few concluding remarks should be made before the Vedic data is taken into consideration. Since Helen is rendered the daughter of that (νέμεσις "divine retribution") which she herself personifies as an instrument in the epic plot, it would not be altogether arbitrary to assume that her role as twin sister of the Dioscuri was a secondary development within the Cyclic tradition, and that her ties of kinship with the Dioscuri was interpreted differently at earlier stages. Helen's role as sister of the Dioscuri and daughter of Zeus and Leda/Nemesis does not give us any obvious reason to compare her fate with that of her mother. A closer look at the features that she shared with other ladies in Greek mythology does bring her somewhat closer to a set of overlapping themes with which the story of the rape of Nemesis

[103] Clader 1976: 54.

is loosely associated: that of rape (more specifically the rape-from-χορός episodes discussed by Boedeker), shape-shifting, and different properties of the goddess Eos. In her role as chorus-leader of the Leukippides and as patron of the young maidens of Sparta, Helen may have been closely linked to Eos or the "Dawn-goddess" Aotis; Helen was abducted (αἱρέω) by Theseus from a χορός while dancing as a maiden in the honor of Artemis, and in a similar context Thetis (possibly while performing a ring-dance) was abducted (αἱρέω) by Peleus from a χῶρος, transforming herself into an animal as a stratagy to escape her pursuer. The latter motif is likewise conspicuous in the description of Nemesis and Zeus.

The purpose of joining together this chain of thematic links, which weakens as we add more links to it, is not to demonstrate that it necessarily constitutes an organic whole. In so far as analogies of these kinds are approached synchronically, we may explain the similarity in different but likewise compelling fashions (some of which need not imply that the analogies are historically interdependent). Still, to use the words of Jonathan Z. Smith, "there is nothing 'natural' about the enterprise of comparison. Similarity and difference are not 'given'. They are the result of mental operations."[104] If we want to study a motif (or a set of motifs) from a diachronic point of view, on the other hand, thematic links may serve as important clues to the evolutionary process, but they are far from exhaustive when it comes to approaching the gradual change and ramification of the motif. A diachronic perspective requires that additional attention is paid to the level of diction, which in this case also involves the etymology of the nouns, proper nouns, verbs, etc. characteristic of certain modes of expression.

Émile Benveniste once made the important remark that the languages historically characterized as "Indo-European" have certain

---

[104] Smith 1990: 51.

obvious structural traits in common, but that the conjunction of structural traits *beyond history* does not suffice for defining such languages as Indo-European.[105] In the historical study of language, just as in the historical study of myth, it is also necessary to consider the formal aspects of the comparanda, which essentially means going *beyond the structural traits*. As a social fact, myth has both structure and form, theme and diction, it has a purpose in the present and bears the marks of the past in which it changed and took shape. It is the purpose of the following investigation to outline a possible trajectory of the motifs studied so far: the conception and birth of the Dioscuri, the relation between Helen and the Disocuri, and Helen's association with Eos.

## *Heaven's Incest*

Since the earliest days of comparative mythology, scholars have assigned a common background to the Greek Dioscuri and the Vedic Aśvins, or Nāsatyas, the divine twins often referred to in the hymns as *dívo nápātā* "descendants of Dyaus" (cf. Greek Διόσκουροι or the archaic dual Διὸς υἷε, Old Latin *iouiois puclois*, Latvian *dieva dēli*, and Lithuanian *diẽva sūnẽlai*[106]).[107] The equation has in fact remained widely accepted up to the present-day. Particularly conspicuous among the features shared by these divine pairs are their

---

105 Problèmes de linguistique générale, Paris 1966: 110.

106 On the basis of the Greek and Lithuanian evidence, we may cautiously argue for an underlying **di̯u̯ós suHnúh*$_1$. The construction **di̯u̯ós* + SONS is in any case inherited.

107 A comprehensive study of the Greek and Vedic parallels appeared in 1876, L. Myriantheus' *Die Aśvins oder arischen Dioskuren* (Munich). The Baltic material was initially discussed by W. Mannhardt in an article from 1875, "Die lettische Sonnenmythen," *Zeitschrift für Ethnologie* 7, 73-104, 209-244, 281-329.

equine,[108] nuptial, and soteriological[109] aspects. They woo or marry a solar female, preferably a daughter of the Sun-god,[110] and appear as companions of the Dawn-goddess. They are healers and helpers, travelling in miraculous vehicles, and rescuing shipwrecked mortals.[111] I have no intention of giving another general survey of these topics here—this has already been done exhaustively by others[112]—but rather to reconsider some problems regarding the conception and birth of the twins.

The confusing state of transmitted data concerning the descent of the Aśvins in the Vedic hymns can easily be grasped by glancing through entries under the heading "Aśvin. Geburt, Familie" in Geldner's "Namenindex": "vom Himmel geboren [...], Enkel des Himmels [...], als ein Paar geboren [...], Sindhu ihre Mutter [...], der eine Sohn des Sumakha, der andere als Sohn des Himmels [...], Uṣas ihre Mutter [...], ihre Geburt an verschieden Orte [...], Zwillinge."

While some of the terms translated here are ambiguous, the apparent confusion may of course be due to an insufficient understanding of the terms and the different contexts in which they occur. It may be wrong, for instance, to interpret *dívo nápātā* in RV[113] 4,44,2b as meaning "Enkel des Himmels," especially since the same poet in a preceeding hymn (4,43) refers to the pair as *divá ā́jātā* (3c) "born

---

[108] Cf. Vedic *aśvin-* "possessing horses" and the Dioscuri as ἱππόται σοφοί (Alcman), εὔιπποι (Pindar), λευκόπωλοι (Pindar), etc.

[109] Cf. *nā́satya-* (probably a so-called "Vr̥ddhibildung" based on a deverbative noun **nas-ati* from √*NAS* "return (safely) home") and κάλλιστοι σωτῆρες (Terpander), etc.

[110] Cf. Vedic Sūryā (occasionally *sū́ryasya duhitár-* or *sū́ras duhitár-*) and Latvian *saules meita.*

[111] The latter theme is of passim occurrence in the Vedic hymns, but compare also *the Homeric Hymn to the Dioscuri* (33).

[112] A recent treatment is found in Cheryl Steets' 1993 UCLA dissertation "The Sun Maiden's Wedding: An Indo-European Sunrise/Sunset Myth" (with references to earlier research on pages 35-39).

[113] If not otherwise stated, all references in this chapter are to the *Rig Veda* (RV).

from Dyaus."[114] To a certain extent, however, we must expect this tradition to contain inconsistencies, at least if the evidence is taken at face value. This is far from surprising, because large portions of the corpus of Vedic hymns fall into a number of subdivisions (the so called "Family Books"), which were composed and handed down by members of priestly families over a long period of time. Shifting theological and mythological views may thus simply be due to local variations and, since this collection contains material extending over several centuries, some differences may also be due to gradual changes over time. There is consequently no reason to expect perfect consistency in this highly diversified and temporally layered collection of hymns. Furthermore, just as words and acts may change their meaning in a ritual setting, a changing ritual context may eventually affect the interpretation of mythical conditions and relations. Nevertheless, the elusive charcter of the data need not induce us to abandon every search for symmetry and consistency. As long as this symmetry is not forced on the material, such a search still appears as the most productive and promising approach.

There is a shred of evidence in some Vedic passages suggesting that the Aśvins (or at least one of them) were the sons of Dyaus and Uṣas.[115] Looking more closely at this evidence can be productive. In fact, ge-

---

[114] Although *nápāt-* could mean "grandson" in certain contexts (a clear-cut example is 10,10,1: "he should provide the father with a *nápāt-*"), the term undoubtedly had a broader sense. The less specific sense "descendant" is often more appropriate, and in some cases the term is apparently exchangeable with terms meaning "son." For instance, *ū́rjo napāt* (= Agni) (1,58,8d, etc) could hardly have meant "grandson of force" in light of the analogous epithets of Agni *ūrjáḥ putrám* (1,96,3c) "son of force," *sūno sahaso* (1,58,8a, etc.) "son of power," and *sáhasas putró* (2,7,6c, etc.) "id."

[115] Cf. Nagy 1990: 256: "Accordingly, the two of them together are the sons of *Dyáus* 'Sky' (1,182,1) and the sons of Uṣas (3,39,3, to be supplemented by the comments of Sāyana concerning this passage)." Cf. also Geldner's commentary to RV 1,181,4 (footnote 1): "Der andere der Aśvin entstammt darnach wohl der bekannten Verbindung des Himmels mit der Tochter Uṣas."

nealogical information concerning the links between the Aśvins, Dyaus, and Uṣas falls into five different (possibly overlapping) categories, which can all be supported by direct textual evidence:

1. Both twins are the sons/descendants of Dyaus
2. Both twins are the sons of Uṣas
3. One of the twins is the son of Dyaus
4. One of the twins is the son of Uṣas
5. Uṣas is the sister of the Aśvins

The evidence is as follows:

1. Both twins are the sons/descendants of Dyaus: This information may be encapsulated in the recurrent appelative *divó nápātā*, but since *nápāt-* could be understood in more general terms as "descendant" (or more specifically "grandson"), I would also quote *divá ā́jātā* (4,43,3c) (see above). To the best of my knowldge, the Aśvins are never called *putrā́ divás* or *sūnū́ divás* (but see below [3]).

2. Both twins are the sons of Uṣas: The main evidence is 3,39,3. The first two stanzas of the hymn (to Indra) are concerned with the emergence of poetic inspiration at dawn. The poem, "fashioned into an eulogy" (*stómataṣṭa-*) (1b) and "wakeful" (*jā́gr̥vi-*) (1c, 2d), reaches Indra from the heart of the poet (1ab) as an adorned spouse (2c). An underlying theme is apparently the evocation of the Dawn-goddess as a patron of poetic inspiration, whose appearance in the early morning signals the commencement of ritual performances. The performance of rites in the early morning is clearly attested in the Vedic hymns. The Indo-European background of this convention is possibly reflected by the Latin verb *iaiientāre* (**Hiaǵ-i̯u-*) "to have breakfast," which may belong to the family of Vedic *yajati*,

ἅζομαι, etc. (√*Hiaǵ*) "to worship."[116] Just as Uṣas (or the song that she inspires) "awakens" (√*JAR* [< PIE √*$h_1ger$]), √*BODH*) gods and mortals in the early morning (cf. 3,58,1: *uṣása stómo aśvínāv ajīgaḥ* "the eulogy of Uṣas has awakened the two Aśvins"), the poem that emerges from the poet's heart at dawn may be characterized as "wakeful" (*jā́gr̥vi-*, from the intensive stem *jā́gr̥-* [< *$h_1$gé-$h_1$gr̥-*]). A similar employment of the cognate verb ἐγείρω (< √*$h_1ger$) is seen in Greek poetics. Just as Eos awakens the sleeper (cf. *Od.* 6,48: Αὐτίκα δ' Ἠὼς ἦλθεν ἐύθρονος, ἥ μιν ἔγειρε / Ναυσικιάαν), a new poem may be "awakened" (ἐγείρω) by the Muse or some other medium of inspiration (e.g. Pindar *Ol.* 9,47; *Pyth.* 9,104; *Nem.* 10,21; Fr. 6a).[117] Accordingly, the focus in the following stanza (3,39,3) is very likely Uṣas herself (an interpretation supported both by Geldner and the indigenous commentator Sāyaṇa[118]):

> yamā́ cid átra yamasū́r asūta ˈ jihvā́yā ágram pátad ā́ hy ásthāt |
> vápūṃṣi jātā́ mithunā́ sacete ˈ tamohánā tápuṣo budhná étā ||
> "Even here, the birth-giver of twins gave birth to twins – verily, the flying thought has entered upon the tip of the tongue. Born as a pair, they (the Aśvins?) accompany the wonders. Smashers of darkness, having gone after (lit. 'on the ground of'[119]) the embers."

The characterization of the Aśvins as "smashers of darkness" (*tamohánā*) underscores the notion of the twins arriving in their wagon at dawn. As seen elsewhere (10,40,12c), the adjective *mithuná-* "paired" – here in the bipartite formula "born as a pair" (*jatā́ mithunā́*) – elsewhere applies to the Aśvins (*ábhūtaṃ gopā́ mithunā́ śubhas patī* "you

[116] Forssman 1993: 100f., Mayrhofer EWAia, s.v. YAJ.

[117] The topic is treated at more lenght in Jackson 2006.

[118] Cf. Geldner (vol. 1, p. 381, footnote 3a) who criticizes Oldenberg's idea that the "twins" correspond to the generic categories *ŕ̥c* and *sā́man*.

[119] According to Geldner, *budhná* "ground" is used here in the locative case as a temporal preposition (cf. elsewhere (7,15,5c) *ágre* "on the tip" used in the opposite temporal sense "before").

[Aśvins] became two paired sheperds [= protectors], you lords of beauty") although it usally implies a male and female component.

3. One of the twins is the son of Dyaus: The notion that one of the twins was the son of Dyaus is explicit in 1,181,4, which develops an attested idea (5,73,4c) that the twins were born on different locations (*nā́nā jātā́v arepásā* "born, stainless, each individually/here and there"):

> ihéha jātā́ sám avāvaśītām ˈ arepásā tanvā̀ nā́mabhiḥ svaíḥ I
> jiṣṇúr vām anyáh súmakhasya sūrír ˈ divó anyáḥ subhágaḥ putrá ūhe II
> "born here and there they, the two stainless ones have striven together with body and with their names. The one of you, the victorious lord/sacrificial patron, is (the son) of Sumakha, the other is called the well-supplied son of Dyaus."

As often noticed by students of the Dioscuric tradition, the separate descent of each twin in Vedic is suggestive of the idea, first attested in the *Cypria* (Fr. 6, Davies) and in Pindar (*Nemean,* 10,79ff.), that Polydeukes was the immortal son of Zeus,[120] and Kastor the mortal son of Tyndareus. It is also significant that, in both traditions and despite the apparent paradox, both twins are referred to as descendants of Dyaus/Zeus.

4. One of the twins is the son of Uṣas: Another version of the notion discussed above (3) maintains that the twins, instead of having different fathers, had different mothers (one of which was Uṣas). It is found in the etymological treatise by Yāska (12,1), who quotes an unidentified Vedic source: "the one (of the Aśvins) is called Vāsātya,

---

[120] The reference to Polydeukes as a "scion of Ares" (ὄζος Ἄρηος) should probably not be understood in genealogical terms, but rather as an epithet of a famous warrior (cf. LSJ, s.v. ὄζος).

the other is your son, o Uṣas" (*vāsātyo*[121] *anya ucyate uṣaḥ putras tavānya*).

5. Uṣas is the sister of the Aśvins: The idea of Uṣas as a sister of the Aśvins is actually mentioned in a hymn (1,180,1-2) ascribed to the author Agastya. Agastya is also supposed to have composed one of the stanzas treated above (3), so in this case we could not be dealing with traditions belonging to different schools of interpretation. In 1,180,1d, the Aśvins accompany the Uṣasas (the Dawns or reappearing Dawn[122]) while drinking of the sweet (drink) (*mádhvaḥ píbantā uṣásaḥ sacethe*), and in the second verse of the following stanza (2c) Uṣas is most likely the intended subject: "when the sister shall carry you two" (*svásā yád vāṃ* [...] *bhárāti*). The occasional use of Vedic √*BHAR* "to carry" in the sense "to be pregnant" (cf. also the Young Avestan feminine noun *barəθrī-* "bearer, mother") may be relevant to this passage, especially in considering another passage regarding the birth of the Aśvins treated below.

If we were to analyze this information in a strictly genealogical fashion, assuming that we are not merely dealing with independent and contradictory variants, certain questions arise: how could Uṣas be both daughter of Dyaus, mother of the son(s) of Dyaus, and sister of the sons of Dyaus? If she is the daughter of Dyaus, she would cer-

---

121 Regarding the name Vāsātya, we cannot avoid noticing an echo of the proper noun Nāsatya, which in Epic literature could be used as the name of one of the Aśvins (in Vedic always in the dual to denote both Aśvins). The verbal roots forming the basis of the noun *vāsātya-* would either be VAS$^2$ "to shine, flash" or VAS$^3$ "to reside, linger, stay overnight." The former root is also contained in the names Uṣas and Vivasvat. The formation of the noun is comparable to that of *nā́satya-*, **nas-atí-* taking Vṛddhi on the model of *vas-atí-* (√*VAS*$^3$) "habitation" (cf. Mayrhofer EWAia, s.v. *nā́satya-*).

122 The alteration between plural and singular designations is not uncommon in the case of Uṣas. It was probably motivated by the daily reappearence of dawn.

tainly be the sister or half-sister of the sons of Dyaus, but how could she then be their mother, and if she is their mother, how could she be their sister? The only solution to this apparent riddle is to assume that she was the victim of incest. This would also render the ambiguous epithet *nápātā* more understandable, for in the case of incest, the twins would simultaneously be the sons of the daughter of Dyaus, hence the grandsons of Dyaus, and the sons of Dyaus.

Students of myth may consider such assumptions absurd, because it lies in the nature of myth to violate intuitions about objects and beings in our own environment. While there is some truth in this, myths often exist in a number of variants and convey counter-intuitive information, they would be virtually incomprehensible if this was always and invariably the case. It would of course be ill-considered to presuppose divine incest on the mere basis of genealogical inconsistencies in some discrete textual passages, but in this particular case, a myth of incest involving Uṣas and her own father is in fact extant. Although the Aśvins are not explicitly associated with this myth, some details in (and post-Vedic renderings of) another, apparently isolated story treating the conception and birth of the Aśvins, makes the assumption compelling that these traditions were somehow interdependent. First let us consider the story of Heaven's incest and its different reflexes in Vedic literature.

The myth is more or less exhaustively developed in the Rigveda. A slightly altered version occurs in the Brāhmaṇas as a focus of ritual exegesis and aetiological speculation. The following presentation of some Vedic sources in translation follows the example of Stephanie Jamison, who gives an excellent survey of the topic in her book *The Ravenous Hyenas and the Wounded Sun.*[123] Although I have chosen a slightly different line of argument here, it should be emphasized that the complexity of Vedic mythology does not per-

---

[123] Jamison 1991. See especially chapter E. (288ff.) "What Did the Sun Do Wrong?"

mit definite or exclusive interpretations of single myths. The major Rigvedic clues[124] to the story of "Heaven's incest" are listed here in their order of appearance, followed by two variants attested in the same collection:

1,71,5
mahé yát pitrá īṃ rásaṃ divé kár ' áva tsarat pr̥śanyàś cikitvā́n |
sr̥jád ástā dhr̥ṣatā́ didyúm asmai ' svā́yāṃ devó duhitári tvíṣiṃ dhāt ||
"When he (Agni) had prepared sap for great father Dyaus, he (Agni) sneaked away, having perceived the caresses (of Dyaus and Uṣas?). The archer (Agni/Rudra) boldly released a missile at him (Dyaus), when the god carried out his 'arousal' on his own daughter." [125]

6,12,4d
'usraḥ[126] pitéva jārayā́yi
"[...] as the father caressed (became the lover of) Uṣas [...]"[127]

---

[124] I have excluded 3,31,1-3, because it seems too vague in this regard.

[125] The translation of the second verse follows Jamison (296) with the exception of the last hemistich. Jamison's interpretation of *tvíṣi-* ("he placed his 'brilliance' in his own daughter") does not seem necessary in this context, because the underlying verb √*TVEṢ* could also imply a state of arousal (cf. EWAia, s.v. √*TVEṢ*)—cf. also LIV (s.v. **tu̯eis* "erregen, erschüttern"), where *tvíṣ(i)-* is taken to mean either "Erregung" or "Funkeln"). Since Sūrya (who may have been associated with a similar transgression) is not explicitly mentioned in this stanza, it seems more natural to interpret the noun in terms of the (formulaic) "desire" of Prajāpati as emphasized in latter renderings of the same myth (see below). I have instead followed Geldner's suggestion here: "Der Gott verrichtete seine Brunst an der eigenen Tochter."

[126] The *r*-stem *usŕ̥-* is closely related to the proper noun Uṣas, and should probably be treated as a synonym, or variant of the name.

[127] Although supported in earlier research by Grassman and Geldner, this translation is debatable. If *jārayā́yi* is derived from √*JAR* "awake" rather than *jārá-* "lover," the passage would evoke the different notion of the father "being awakened by Dawn" (cf. Meillet "il a été éveillé par le sacrifices comme le père de l'Aurore") (Stephanie Jamison, personal communication).

10,61,5-8
5. práthiṣṭa yásya vīrákarman iṣṇád ' ánuṣṭiaṃ nú nāryo ápauhat I
púnas tád ā́ vr̥hati kanā́yā ' duhitúr ā́ ánubhr̥tam anarvā́ II 6. madhyā́ yát kartvam ábhavad abī́ke ' kā́maṃ kr̥ṇvāné pitári yuvatyā́m I manānág réto jahatur viyántā ' sā́nau níṣiktaṃ sukr̥tasya yónau II 7. pitā́ yát svā́ṃ duhitáram adhiṣkán ' kṣmayā́ rétaḥ saṃjagmānó ní ṣiñcat I svādhyò 'janayan bráhma devā́ ' vā́stoṣ pátṃ vratapā́ṃ nír atakṣan II 8. sá īṃ vŕ̥ṣā ná phénam asyad ājaú ' smád ā́ páraid ápa dabhrácetāḥ I sárat padā́ ná dákṣiṇā parāvŕ̥ṅ ' ná tā́ nú me pr̥śaṇyò jagr̥bhre II

"5. (The one) whose (penis, which) performs the manly work, stretched out, discharging (the seed)—that one, the manly one, then pulled away (his penis, which had been) 'attending on/following' (her). He tore out again from the maiden, his daughter, what (had been) thrust in—the unmastered.[128] 6. As it happened, in the midst of the act, during the intercourse of father and maiden, a little seed got lost when they went apart, which poured down on the back (of the earth), on the abode of good deeds (= the ritual ground?). 7. When the father 'sprang upon' his own daughter, uniting with her, he poured down seed on the earth.[129] Piously the gods generated a form(ulation) and fashioned thereof Vāstoṣpati (= the 'lord of the abode', an epithet of Rudra), the lord of the law. 8. Like a bull in a fight, he (Dyaus?) ejected foam. Hence and forth he went (being) out of his mind. Like an outcast she (Uṣas) hastened to the southern regions (saying) 'the caresses have not been successful.'"

Variant 1
1,164,33
dyaúr me pitā́ janitā́ nā́bhir átra ' bándhur me mātā́ pr̥thivī mahī́yám I
uttānáyos camvòr yónir antár ' átrā pitā́ duhitúr gárbham ā́dhāt II
"Heaven/Dyaus (is) my father and procreator[130], here is the/my navel. The Mother Earth/Pr̥thivī (is) a relation of mine. Between the two outstretched

[128] Tr. Jamison 1997: 296
[129] Tr. Jamison, ibid.
[130] The hereditary features of the formula *dyaúr me pitā́ janitā́* are briefly discussed above.

(Soma-)vessels[131] (is) the womb. Here (in the womb) the father placed the embryo of the daughter."[132]

Variant 2
5,42,13
prá sū́ mahé suśaraṇā́ya medhā́ṃ ꞌ gíram bhare návyasīṃ jā́yamānām ꞌ
yá āhanā́ duhitúr vakṣáṇāsu ꞌ rūpā́ minānó ákr̥ṇod idáṃ naḥ ꞌꞌ
"Verily, to the great one providing good shelter (Tvaṣṭr̥/Dyaus[133]), I offer the wisdom (as an) eulogy born anew. He who, lustful/swelling, having damaged the forms in the cavities of the daughter, made this our (form) here."

The chief agents of the myth are not always mentioned by name, but the passages identifying them as Dyaus and Uṣas are by no means contradicted by the other passages. As implied by Geldner in his commentary to 5,42,13, however, Dyaus may occasionally have been replaced by the god Tvaṣṭr̥. This particular ambivalence (or possible shift of focus) in fact provides a clue to the treatment of the myth in some of the later Vedic sources. A conspicuous aspect of both Dyaus and Tvaṣṭr̥ (lit. "fashioner") is their (pro)creative force (cf., for instance, 10,46,9, where both gods occur side by side): Tvaṣṭr̥ produces (or releases) the seed (*turī́pa-*) from which all creatures

131 Probably to be understood metaphorically as "heaven and earth." The whole hymn is a collection of riddles, so called *brahmodyāni*, which formed a part of (and to some extent also concerned) the Vedic ritual.

132 I see no obvious reason to follow Geldner's interpretation here. He takes the daughter to be Pr̥thivī (cf. his commentary to 1,71,5), implying that the quoted stanza relates an alternative version of the myth of Heaven's incest.

133 The twice attested *suśaraṇá-* is once specifically associated with Tvaṣṭr̥ (7,34,22cd), which suggests that he is the object of offering in this stanza. Geldner gives the following motivation "Die Tochter des Tvaṣṭr̥ ist das Urweib, aus dem er die einzelnen Formen schafft. Die Schöpfung beruht also auf einem Inzest. Tvaṣṭr̥ ist das männliche, seine Tochter das weibliche Schöpfungsprinzip." Since the same adjective (without the adverb *sú*) is also associated with *dyáv-* (*śaraṇé divó* "in the shelter of the sky" [8,25,19a]), Dyaus would be a fitting candidate as well.

are born (1,142,10; 3,4,9); Tvaṣṭr̥ extends the offspring/creatures (*prajā́ḥ*), creating (*jajāna*) them in great number (3,55,19); he who offers to Dyaus and Pr̥thivī "propagates himself through offspring" (*prá prajā́bhir jā́yate*, 6,70,3c); Soma brings forth the creatures (*prajā́*) from the "seed of Heaven" (*divyàsya rétasas*, 9,86,28), etc.

This common feature of Dyaus and Tvaṣṭr̥, indexed by the verb *pra+√JAN* "to flourish, propagate" and the derivative noun *prajā́-* "offspring, creature," is crystalized in the epithet *prajā́pati-* "lord of creatures," which either denotes a god in his own right (only in the late Rigveda) or functions as an epithet of other gods (e.g. Soma [9,5,9] or Savitar [4,53,2]).[134] In the younger strata of Vedic literature, however, Prajāpati achieves a prominent status as the god or primal being who "emits" the world through a sacrificial act.[135] It is difficult to decide if this literature testifies to the emergence of a "new god" and to what extent this god could have incorporated aspects of other Vedic gods, but later treatments of the myth of Heaven's incest undoubtedly identified the father of Uṣas as Prajāpati. In one of these texts (Śatapatha Brāhmaṇa 1,7,4,3-4), a Rigvedic passage (10,61,7) relating the myth of Heaven's incest is even quoted verbatim. We need not hesitate, therefore, in asserting that the Maitrāyaṇī Saṃhitā and some of the Brāhmaṇas contain the *same* myth as the one attested in the Rigveda (albeit with Prajāpati as perpetrator instead of Dyaus). It is reasonable to assume that some of the details in the earlier versions of the myth were already implicit in the Rigvedic versions. One such detail is the tranformation of Uṣas and Prajāpati into animals. Although this motif is found in most of the later versions, the Rigveda only vaguely hints in this regard (cf. the verb *ádhi+√SKAND* "to mount, spring upon" in 10,61,7a, which would chiefly apply to animals, or the possible reference to Dyaus behaving "like a bull" [*vŕ̥ṣā ná*] in 10,61,8a).

---

134 Jamison 1990: 293.

135 Malamoud 1996: 59ff.

The following are the basic versions of earlier treatments of the myth. I quote Jamison's translations:

MS 3,6,5
"Prajāpati 'approached' his own daughter, Dawn (Uṣas). His seed flew forth. The gods approached (it) together (...and) picked it up... With it they stretched the worship."

MS 4,2,12
"Prjāpati desired his own daughter, Dawn (Uṣas). She became a red doe. He, having become a buck, 'approached' her. It seemed 'against commandment' to him (Rudra). He (Rudra) turned toward him (Prajāpati) with an outstreched (arrow). He (Prajāpati), feared him (Rudra) and said, 'I will make you lord of beasts, but don't stand against me.' [...] (Rudra), on taking aim, pierced him. He cried out (a*rod*īt). And that is his name: *Rudra* [...] The first seed that flew forth was kindled by the fire [...] The (seed) that overflowed Bṛhaspati collected."

ŚB 1,7,4,1-3
"1. Prajāpati longed for his own daughter, either Heaven or Dawn. Thinking, 'Might I make a pair with her,' he united with her. 2. To the gods this was a sin: 'Who does thus to his own daughter, our sister (commits a sin).' 3. The gods said to this god who is Master of Beasts (Rudra), 'this one violates custom(ary law) who does thus to his own daughter, our sister. Pierce him!' Rudra on taking aim, pierced him. Half of his seed spilled forth."

AB 3,33
"Prajāpati longed for his own daughter—some say 'Heaven,' others 'Dawn.' Having become a buck, he 'approached' her, who had become a red doe. The gods saw, 'Prajāpati does (something) not to be done.' They sought one who would harm him. They did not find anyone among themselves. They collected together into their own most dreadful bodies. Thus collected, they became this god [= Rudra] [...] The gods said to him, 'this Prajāpati has done (something) not to be done. Pierce him!'[...] Having taken aim, he pierced him. Pierced, he flew straight up [...] The seed (which had) poured from Prajāpati, flowed."

JB 3,262-263
"262. [...] Prajāpati longed for his own daughter, Dawn. She having become a red doe, stood (still?) for him. He, having become a speckled deer, spilled (his seed) on her. He ('the noninjurious god') saw, 'for this did the gods create me, for overseeing. This one transgresses. Well, I will pierce him.' He (Prajāpati), pierced, having thrown away his form, strode straight up [...] 263. Of him, pierced, the seed flew forth."

As demonstrated by Jamison, it is easy to recognize formulaic features in all these texts—usually in the beginning and the end of the passages, but sometimes next to each other (as seen in MS 3,6,5)—which could be considered to index the whole myth[136]:

MS 3,6,5
prajā́patir vaí svā́ṃ duhitáram ádhyaid uṣásam tasya rétaḥ párāpatat
"Prajāpati 'approached' his own daughter, Dawn (Uṣas). His seed flew forth."

MS 4,2,12
prajā́patir vaí svā́ṃ duhitáram abhyàkāmayatoṣásaṁ [...] táto yát prathamáṁ rétaḥ parā́patat [...]
"Prjāpati desired his own daughter, Dawn [...] the first seed that flew forth [...]"

ŚB 1,7,4,1-3
prajā́patir ha vaí svā́ṃ duhitáram abhídadhyau / dívam voṣásaṃ [...] tásya sāmí rétaḥ prácaskanda
"Prajāpati longed for his own daughter, either Heaven or Dawn [...] Half of his seed spilled forth."

AB 3,33
prajāpatir vai svāṃ duhitaram abhyadhyāyad divam ity anya āhur uṣasam ity anye [...] tad vā idam prajāpate retaḥ siktam adhavat
"Prajāpati longed for his own daughter—some say 'Heaven', others 'Dawn' [...] The seed (which had) poured from Prajāpati, flowed."

136 Jamison 1997: 128f.

JB 3,262;263
prajāpatir hoṣasaṃ svāṃ duhitaram abhyadhyāyat [...] tasya viddhasya retaḥ parāpatat
"Prajāpati longed for his own daughter, Dawn [...] Of him, pierced, the seed flew forth."

The formal agreements are in fact so striking that we can reconstruct an underlying sentence, summarizing the essentials of the myth as implied by the emphatic particle *vai* (in all versions exept for JB, which instead has the enclitic *ha*). The unisonant, metrically identical members *prajā́patis* and *párāpatat* seem to form a ring, evoking the god whose principal function is to emit/let flow forth (*parā+√PAT*) the essence of living creatures (*prajā́-*):

**prajā́patir svā́m duhitáram (abhi)√DHAY* ("to devise" → "to desire"), *uṣásam, tásya rétaḥ párāpatat*

Similar features are also discernible in the Rigveda, repeating and summarizing a more detailed description found in other hymns, or elsewhere in the same hymn:

10,61,7ab
pitā́ yát svā́ṃ duhitarā́ram adhiṣkán ǀ kṣmayā́ rétaḥ saṃjagmānó ní ṣiñcat
"when the father 'sprang upon' his own daughter, uniting with her, he poured down seed on the earth"

1,71,5d
svā́yāṃ devó duhitári tvíṣiṃ dhāt
"when the god carried out his 'arousal' on his own daughter"

Despite the formal traits of its many variants, the story (or rather exegesis) of Heaven's/Prajāpati's incest developed in a number of different ways. The most ambiguous aspect of the story seems to be the outcome of the transgression. Most versions tend to agree on the point that the father's desire for his own daughter is to be considered a sin. The other gods try to prevent the felony by releasing a missile at the father, sometimes by creating an intermediary agent to perform the task. Another notion shared by most of the versions is that the transgression, despite being objectionable as such, still had a positive outcome (such as the creation of life). Gonda regards this mythical narrative as "a variant of the widespread theme of the *Urinzest*, the primeval incestuous creation of living beings, and a variant of the theme of the adversary or antagonist,"[137] but pays no attention to the apparent fact that the other gods considered Prajāpati (or Dyaus) to be commiting sin.

According to some older versions of the story (RV 1,71,8 and AB 3,34,1), the natural outcome of the forbidden union between Uṣas and her father was a group of semi-divine beings, the prototypical poet-priest known as the Aṅgirases (often seven in number). These poet-priests assist Indra in releasing the cows of Dawn from their imprisonment in the cave of Vala by performing exemplary rituals, i.e. by initializing and motivating future ritual performances. They are the fathers of humankind (*pitáro manuṣyā̀*, 4,1,13a), but also achieve divine status (or reach heaven) through the power of their pious acts (5,15,3). To the best of my knowledge, the Aśvins are never mentioned in direct association with the myth of Heaven's incest. They are indeed mentioned alongside Uṣas in a stanza (10,61,4) preceding the most extensive treatment of the myth in the Rigveda. It is possible that this stanza anticipates the myth as a whole, but nowhere are the Aśvins explicitly said to be the offspring of Dyaus and Uṣas within the framework of this particular myth. True, the Aśvins were occasionally treated as the sons or descendants of Dyaus and the sons and/or sibblings of Uṣas. But there is no passage to suggest that the union between Dayus and Uṣas was more than a unique transgression. While such conclusions are purely inductive,

[137] Gonda 1986: 74.

the lack of other clues would make these conclusions less persuasive in the context of myth. The discovery of such clues requires a detour. A possible missing link is found in an alternative rendering of the Aśvins' descent, the post-Vedic treatment of which brings us back to the myth of Heaven's incest, the transformation of the cohabitants into animals, and the spilling of semen on the ground.

## *The Story of Sarayṇyū*

The earliest attested allusion to this story occurs in the tenth book of the Rigveda (10,17,1-2). It is condensed into two enigmatic stanzas, apparently referring to an incomplete wedding ceremony, from which the bride, the mother of the Aśvins and mortal Yama, suddenly disappears. The gods (or some group of gods) hide her from the mortals by making a copy of her, a *sávarṇa-* ("same appearance"), which is given to the bridegroom in her place:

1. tváṣṭā duhitré vahatúṃ kr̥ṇoti ˈ ítīdám víśvam bhúvanaṃ sám eti ǀ
yamásya mātā́ paryuhyámānā ˈ mahó jāyā́ vívasvato nanāśa ǁ

2. ápāgūhann amŕ̥tām mártyebhyaḥ ˈ kr̥tvī́ sávarṇām adadur vívasvate ǀ
utā́śvināv abharad yát tád ā́sīd ˈ ájahād u dvā́ mithunā́ saraṇyū́h ǁ

"1. 'Tvaṣṭr arranges a wedding for his daughter' by this (utterance) the whole world comes together. The mother of Yama, brought home (as) the bride of great Vivasvat, disappeared. 2. They (the gods?) hid away the immortal from mortals. Having made one of same appearance, they gave her to Vivasvat. And she carried the two Aśvins when that happened. And she left the two behind as a pair, Saraṇyū."

Save for a possible allusion to the daughter of Tvaṣṭr̥ (5,42,13) and a reference to the mother of Manu (Sāvarṇī) (10,62,11), the two stanzas do not bear any obvious relation to other Vedic passages. The stanzas are repeated separately in AV (18,1,53 and 18,2,33) without any conspicuous divergences or further clues as to their background. The proper noun "Saraṇyū" is also attested in a Rigvedic apocryphe, a so-called *Khila* (11,5), where it denotes (once more in apposition) the mother of the Aśvins entering their wagon (*yád vām mātā́ úpa ā́tiṣṭhad ugraṃ suvṛdráthaṃ avyatheyáṃ saráṇyūḥ*).[138] The adjective *saraṇyú-* is attested four times in the Rigveda, and we can be reasonably sure that it meant "hasty, quick" (→ √*SAR* "to rush, run away, hasten").[139] Other passages confirm that Vivasvat was the father of Yama and Manu, but (as indicated in 10,62,11) Saraṇyū was not regarded as the mother of Manu.

Most interpreters (ranging from Sāyaṇa to modern scholars such as Geldner and Elizarenkova) have taken *dvā́ mithunā́* in 2d as a reference to the twins Yama and Yamī. This interpretation is suggested by other, albeit much later versions of the same story, and by the fact that the dual *mithunā́* usually denotes a pair consisting of a male and a female. As indicated above, however, clear exceptions to this rule are the passages associating the Aśvins with this adjective (notably 3,39,3c [also in the context of pregnancy and birth] and 10,40,12c). Another good reason for taking *dvā́ mithunā́* in 2d as a reference to the Aśvins is the fact that they are the only twins explicitly referred to in the verse. A third possibility would be to take *dvā́ mithunā́* as "two pairs of twins" (instead of "the two, as a pair"), which would then imply a reference to the two Aśvins and Yama/Yamī or Yama/Manu.[140] This suggestion seems rather unlikely. Likewise improbable is the argument that the verb *ájahād* could not have meant "aban-

---

[138] Cf. the emmendtations in J. Scheftelowitz' edition 1906: 67. A similar motif, with similar wording, involves the Aśvins and the "daughter of Sūrya" in the Rigveda proper (*ā vā́ṃ ráthaṃ duhitā́ sū́ryasya ˈ kā́rṣmevātiṣṭhad árvatā jáyantī*, 1,116,17ab).

[139] Cf. the figura etymologica *sárat saráṇyúḥ* in 10,61,23b.

[140] Steets 1993: 46f.

doned" but rather "left behind (for posterity)" if it were to include the Aśvins, "because Saraṇyū only abandoned the first set, Yama and his twin, she did not abandon the Aśvins, who were born subsequent to her disappearance."[141] This way of reasoning is circular, because it derives from texts using the Rigvedic passage as their main source, not the other way around. The Rigvedic passage does not mention the twin sister of Yama, nor Yama's putative twin brother Manu (who is only associated with Yama in later sources), nor does it exclude the possibility that the Aśvins could have been abandoned by their mother. Furthermore, it hardly appears from what is said in 2c that the Aśvins should be taken as being either carried or born by Saraṇyū subsequent to her disappearance. I would suggest that the expression *yát tád ā́sīd* is clearly deictic with regard to one, some, or all of the events mentioned in the preceding verses, implying that Saraṇyū carried the Aśvins *when that happened*, on the occasion of this or that event referred to in a preceding verse. In other words, that she was already pregnant at the time of her wedding. Cheryl Steets instead takes this expression to mean "when this had happened,"[142] but does not explain why the imperfect *ā́sit* should be translated as a pluperfect. If the subsequent birth of the Aśvins constituted the basic message of this expression, we would not expect a verb denoting pregnancy, but rather *ásūta* ("[she] gave birth") or something similar. It seems anomalous to say "she was pregnant when that had happened," since we would rather expect "she was (already) pregnant when that happened," or "she became pregnant when that had happened," or "she gave birth when that had happened." The fact that Saraṇyū is called the "mother of Yama" (*yamásya mātā́*) by no means implies that she gave birth to Yama before giving birth to the Aśvins. From the perspective of the poet, this could just as well ap-

---

[141] Ibid. 47.
[142] Ibid. 43.

ply to her present status, as if one were to say: "before X's mother gave birth to her first child."

It is not unusual for a Vedic stanza to encapsulate distinct mythic events in this fashion. Among the numerous passages implicitly or explicitly "praising the heroic deeds (*vīryà̄*)" of Indra, consider, for instance, the following stanza (2,12,3): "who (Indra), having killed the serpent, let the seven rivers flow, who (Indra) drove out the cows from the hiding place of Vala, who (Indra) has generated fire between two stones [...]" Distinct mythic events are hinted at here, some of which were so well-known that a few words could capture their essence. Among the most familiar events are the slaying of Vṛtra, a giant serpent enclosing the heavenly waters, and the smashing of the Vala-cave. Although these stories were occasionally treated in more detail, they were often simply alluded to in this fashion. Just as in the rhapsodic treatment of Saraṇyū and the abandoned twins, this stanza also ends with a characteristic apposition of the god's name, repeated throughout the whole hymn (with the exception of the last stanza): *sá janāsa índraḥ* "he, you men (lit. 'born ones'), is Indra." Although the episodes alluded to in 10,17,1-2 need not be as disconnected as in the example given above, nothing suggests that we should read the stanzas as if they were presenting an unbroken course of events: Tvaṣṭṛ arranges a wedding for his daughter → the mother of Yama disappeared → they (the gods?) hid the mortal from mortals → she was pregnant with the Aśvins when this happened → she left the two behind as a pair. Consequently, we do not have to assume that the last hemistich refers to an event immediately following the wedding procedures.

We now turn to the post-Vedic aftermath of the story, keeping in mind that such late renderings may simultaneously alter and preserve older data. The Bṛhaddevatā, a collection of legends from the Fourth century BC based on the Rigvedic hymns, contains narrations of Vedic myths that are occasionally informed by misreadings of the hymns.[143] On the other hand, when Śaunaka (traditionally held to be the author of Bṛhaddevatā) adds data that are neither hinted at in the Rigvedic passage nor triggered by some misreading, it is conceivable that he got them from traditions that were already implicit in the Vedic hymns. As we shall see below, Śaunaka adds data to the story of Saraṇyū that do not seem to fit the events hinted at in the Rigvedic passage. Nevertheless, while these data do not seem to have entered the plot without reason, they may prove suggestive to the overall understanding of the myth. According to the Bṛhaddevatā (6,33-7,6), Saraṇyū gives birth to the twins Yama and Yamī before departing from Vivasvat in the shape of a mare, having herself created the *sávarṇā-* in order to delude her husband. Before discovering her trick, Vivasvat begets Manu with the Saraṇyū's *sávarṇa-*. He then pursues his true wife in the shape of a steed, and is approached by her for sexual intercourse. They begin to mate, but in their agitation his semen falls on the ground (*śukraṃ tad apatad bhuvi*, 7,5). Desiring of offspring, Saraṇyū smells the semen. She eventually gives birth to Nāsatya and Dasra, also known as the Aśvins.

Although a theriomorphic subtext is nowhere hinted at in the Rigvedic allusion to the story, it could still have belonged to an earlier tradition. That is not to say that all aspects of this extended version have to be old. The smelling of the semen, for instance, is probably a late addition derived from the popular etymology associating *nā́satya-* with the word *nás-*, "nose." What stands out as particularly odd in this description, however, is that the Aśvins are conceived subsequent to the events regarded as contemporaneous with Saraṇyū's pregnancy in the Rigvedic passage. It is also noteworthy that Saraṇyū disappears on her own initiative in the Bṛhaddevatā, whereas she is hidden away by some intermediary agent in the Rigveda. We may

143 Cf. the story of Traitana and his slaves (*Bṛhaddevatā* 4,21), which undoubtedly (as seen in the light of Iranian evidence) proceeds from a misreading of RV 1,158,5. The topic is treated in Jackson/Oettinger 2002.

thus assume that the active sense in which she "left the two behind" (*ájahād* [...] *dvā́*) originally pertained to an event distinct from her disappearance. Śaunaka, in believing that these actions belonged to the same episode, interpreted both the disappearance and the abandonment of the twins in an active sense.

To summarize my argument, although Śaunaka does not provide any information regarding the reason for Saraṇyū's disappearance, it is possible that he was familiar with early aspects of the story that left no traces in the earliest extant version. It is unclear, however, if he fully understood the importance and position of these traits in the original plot.

Maurice Bloomfield, who wrote a comprehensive article about the Rigvedic passage and its post-Vedic reception, emphasized that Vedic hymns often contain incongruities, and that the succession of facts does not have to correspond to an underlying story.[144] Like many scholars before him, Bloomfield compared the passage with a set of Vedic cosmogonic themes involving divine incest. According to Albrecht Weber, for instance, the first verse in RV 10,17 suggested that Tvaṣṭr intended to marry his own daughter. The whole world thus "comes together" (*sám eti*), not to take part in wedding festivities, but to prevent a felony. He found support for this assumption in the myth of Heaven's/Prajāpati's incest, correctly arguing that Tvaṣṭr "ganz wohl auch als Name des Prajāpati fungieren konnte," but less convincingly concluding that Tvaṣṭr and Vivasvat should be regarded as one and the same.[145] With justification Bloomfield rejected Weber's interpretation as far-fetched, and also emphasized that "the passages portraying the cosmic incest do not present a single allusion to wedding rites."[146] Nevertheless, Bloomfield still believed that the cosmogonic themes to which Weber referred could

---

[144] Bloomfield 1893: 187.

[145] Weber 1885: vol. 17,310ff.

[146] Bloomfield 1893: 181.

have played an important role in the development of the story of Saraṇyū as it stands, for instance, in the Bṛhaddevatā. He regarded this episode as the result of a compilation "which has combined with considerable fancy a number of mythological and legendary points into a single story."[147] There is good reason to consider Bloomfield's conclusions as more balanced than those of his forerunners. Yet it may be argued that a different and more efficient methodology could be applied to the incongruities. As I will try to show below, it seems possible to inverse Bloomfield's perspective without relying on Weber's argumentation, so that the two verses in RV 10,17 and the passage in the Bṛhaddevatā stand out as the constitutive parts of a dissolving whole. My principal guiding rule in doing so is 1) that the data gathered from different passages in the same corpus are not as a rule contradictory, but rather may appear to be so for lack of sufficient data, and 2) that recurrent vocabulary and phraseology, not only overt thematic parallels, may shed light upon the background of a single motif. This approach could even apply when data are drawn from apparently distinct passages in the same corpus.

It is significant that both Uṣas and Saraṇyū could be regarded as mothers of the Aśvins in the Rigveda, whereas no early text presents Vivasvat as their father. In 10,17,1-2, Vivasvat in fact has very little in common with either Dyaus, or any other god, for he rather resembles a mortal. This would at least explain the sentence in 2a (*ápāgūhann amŕ̥tām mártyebhyaḥ* "they [the gods?] hid away the immortal from mortals"). If Vivasvat was considered a part of this group, it is easy to explain why mortals were attending his wedding. The notion of Vivasvat as a founder of sacrifice (1,139,1; 1,53,1) and a father of mortals (such as Yama [10,14,5; 10,58,1 *et passim*]) suggests a similar status. This also applies to the occurrence of a corresponding figure in Old Iranian literature, Vīuuaŋᵛhaṇt, who is

147 Ibid. 188.

explicitly said to be the "first mortal" (*paoiriiō maṣ̌iiō* [Y 9,4]). Such parallels in Vedic and Old Iranian texts seem to reflect a common Indo-Iranian heritage. According to a well-known Vedic myth, furthermore, Vivasvat was the result of a miscarriage or abnormal birth, a lifeless substance referred to as Mārtāṇḍa "dead egg."[148] The divine nature of Vivasvat, more specifically his role as Sun-god in some texts, could thus be understood as a uniquely Vedic development.[149] On the other hand, the figure identified as the father of Sarayṇyū (Tvaṣṭr̥) does have certain features in common with Dyaus. As suggested by 5,42,13, for instance, he seems to be sharing with Dyaus the role of the father who commits incest with his own daughter.

While Saraṇyū is said to be the mother of mortal Yama, Uṣas is never associated with him. On the other hand, Uṣas is invoked alongside Vivasvat (or rather his nocturnal and diurnal aspects) in 10,39,12, and the onamastic link between Uṣas and Vivasvat—both names probably contain the verbal root *VAS* "to shine, flash" [*$h_2$u̯es*])—suggests that the two figures were sometime conceived as a pair. This does not prove Vivasvat to be the reflex of an immortal Sun-god, because both Uṣas and Saraṇyū adhere to the pattern of the goddess and her mortal lover/husband, a theme underscored by the notion of the mortal twin and his immortal brother. It is also possible that a figure represented as the personified Sun was understood as a mortal. Uṣas is explicitly said to seek mortal lovers (*kás ta uṣaḥ kadhapriye bhujé márto amartye* "what mortal must please you, immortal friend-seeking Uṣas?" [1,30,20ab])[150] and her Greek counterparts, both Eos and Aphrodite, are closely linked to this theme as well.[151]

---

148 For a recent treatment, see Jamison 1991: 204ff.

149 For a different view, see Jamison 1990: 204-208.

150 Tr. Boedeker 1974: 68.

151 Cf. Boedeker 1974: 64-84.

Although a connection between Uṣas and Saraṇyū can only be established on the basis of very limited narrative data, their interdependence may come out differently on the level of diction. It should be emphasized that the diction is not always on a par with the messages composed by means of the same dictional components. We may note, first of all, the thematic, verbal, and prosodic parallelism in the following lines, the first of which concerns Uṣas giving birth to the Aśvins, and the second of which concerns the pregnancy of Saraṇyū and the subsequent abandonment of the twins:

yamā́ cid átra yamasū́r asūta [---] jātā́ mithunā́ sacete (3,39,3)

~

yamásya mātā́ [---] áśvināv abharad [---] ájahād u dvā́ mithunā́ saraṇyū́ḥ (10,17,1-2)

Another compelling clue to the common background of Uṣas and Saraṇyū lies embedded in the proper noun *saraṇyū́-* (√*SAR*).[152] It has occured to others that *saraṇyū́-* would be a fitting epithet of the Dawn-goddess, who is seen to *disappear* when the sun rises.[153] This general, naturalistic characteristic meets with particular and rather concrete feedback in the story of Heaven's incest. It should be kept in mind that myths rarely set out to explain natural phenomena. They are almost never *about* natural object, but rather provide the means to think *with* natural objects and categories.[154] In 10,61,8c, as Dyaus is forced by the other gods to interrupt his desecration of the daughter, Uṣas is said to have "hastened" (*sárat* → √*SAR*) to the southern regions. The same injunctive use of √*SAR* is associated with Uṣas

---

152 The formation of the proper noun is based on the adjective *saraṇyú-* "hasty," which is derived from the verbal present stem *sar-aṇyá-* "to hasten" (cf. also *ukṣaṇyú-* "behaving like a bullock" from the denominative *ukṣaṇ-yá-* [participle *ukṣaṇyánt-*]). I am grateful to Norbert Oettinger for clarifying these points.

153 Pisani 1929 (reprinted in Pisani 1962).

154 Smith 1991: 128f.

elsewhere in the Rigveda. In four stanzas (4,30,8-11) alluding to the insufficently understood story of Indra crushing Uṣas' cart by the river Vipāś, *sárat* and *sasā́ra* even form a ring:

> 8. etád ghéd utá vīryàm ˈ índra cakártha paúṃsiyam |
> stríyaṃ yád durhaṇāyúvaṃ ˈ vádhīr duhitáraṃ diváḥ ||
>
> 9. diváś cid ghā duhitáram ˈ mahā́n mahīyámānām |
> uṣā́sam indra sám piṇak ||
>
> 10. ápoṣā́ ánasaḥ sarat ˈ sámpiṣṭād áha bibhyúṣī |
> ní yát sīṃ śiśnáthad vṛ́ṣā ||
>
> 11. etád asyā ánaḥ śaye ˈ súsampiṣṭaṃ vípāśy ā́ |
> sasā́ra sīm parāvátaḥ ||

"8. Verily, also this heroic deed, (this) manly deed, you have performed, o Indra, when you slayed the malicious woman, Heaven's daughter. 9. Even Heaven's very daughter, Uṣas → [= Uṣas' cart], as she augmented herself [?], you, o mighty one, O Indra, have demolished. 10. Having feared, Uṣas just ran away from the cart, (which was) demolished. When the bull has broken it down. 11. This very cart lies completely demolished in Vipāś. She has fled to the distant regions."

Instead of taking the name "Saraṇyū" as a mythopoeic reflex of natural phenomena, the appellation could be understood as the encapsulation of a single mythic event on the basis of a still flexible set of formulaic constituents. As a distinctive mark of Uṣas in different contexts, the verbal root *SAR* could have underpinned the formation of an epithet, or epiklesis, encapsulating one of the myths in which she took part. The process by means of which intensification of a divine epithet may cause a split in the pantheon is attested elsewhere. In the Roman pantheon, for instance, the name of the goddess Venus probably developed from an epithet or typical attribute of the Indo-European Dawn-goddess, who survived in the Roman pantheon as

Aurora. This hypothethis is made plausible in support of a Vedic ἁπ. λεγ. *vánas-* "desire" (**u̯enos*), which accompanies Uṣas in the Rigvedic hemistich (10,172,1a) *ā́ yāhi vánasā sahá* "come here (Uṣas) with your desire!"[155]

The following examples suggest formal links between the stories of Saraṇyū (A), of Indra crushing Uṣas' cart (B), and of Heaven's incest (C). The conjunction of the two verbal roots *SAR* and *HĀ* in the story of Saraṇyū (A) is echoed in the different versions of the story of Indra crushing Uṣas' cart (C), where the two roots seem more or less replaceable (cf. especially 10,138,5d and 4,30,10a):.

A. *ájahād u dvā mithunā́ saraṇyū́ḥ* (10,17,2d): Saraṇyū (√*SAR*) abandons (√*HĀ* ) her twins.
B1. *chundhyū́r ájahād uṣā́ ánaḥ* (10,138,5d): Uṣas abandons (√*HĀ*) her cart.
B2. *ápoṣā́ ánasaḥ sarat* (4,30,10a): Uṣas flees (√*SAR*), leaving the cart behind.
B3. *sasā́ra sīm parāvátaḥ* (4,30,11c): Uṣas flees (√*SAR*) to the distant regions, leaving her cart behind.
C. *sárat padā́ ná dákṣiṇā* (10,61,8c): Uṣas flees (√*SAR*) to the distant regions, escaping her father.

Implicit references to the story of Heaven's incest in the story of Saraṇyū may be traced in early vocabulary and onomastics as well as in post-Vedic renderings of the story, restating the theme of theriomorphic shape-shifting and the spilled semen. In his treatment of the Vedic story of Saraṇyū, it is possible that Śaunaka was familiar with and wanted to communicate an elsewhere unattested Vedic tradition, but that some of the mythic events and characters associated with this tradition had been confused in the course of their

[155] Dunkel 1990: 10.

transmission. The curious foregrounding of the name "Saraṇyū" in RV 10,17,2d may even suggest that early allusions to the story were intended as aetiologies of the epithet or epiklesis itself, as if providing an answer to the question, "why is Uṣas (or some other goddess) called the 'hasty one'?"

If we were to establish a model from which these different renderings could have developed, both narrative economy and hereditary vocabulary should be taken into account. The center of attraction would be the father (*pitár-*) and procreator (*janitár-* [√*JAN*]) Dyaus (sometimes also Tvaṣṭṛ [+√*JAN*] or Prajāpati [*pra*+√*JAN*]) who desires his own daughter, the Dawn-goddess Uṣas. The two cohabitants transform themselves into animals. Dyaus spills his semen on the ground. Uṣas tries to escape her father and is duly referred to as "hasty" or as "the hasty one" (*saraṇyū́-* [√*SAR*]). As representatives of a lower, semi-divine stratum in the family of gods, the Aśvins are conceived at the event of this incestuous union, but before their birth the father attempts to marry their mother to a mortal. The latter theme develops the familiar association of Uṣas with a mortal lover. Uṣas'/Saraṇyū's premarital pregnancy would, furthermore, explain the bride's disappearance and the creation of the *sávarṇa-*, because girls are expected to be virgins at the time of their marriage.[156] The verb used to denote the hiding of Saraṇyū (*ápāguhann*, 10,17,2a) in fact recurs in a rare Vedic noun (*apagohá-*) that could be used to designate a "hiding-place" where girls hide an undesired, premarital or extra-marital offspring (*apagohám̐ kanī́nām* "girls' hiding-place," 2,15,7a). As suggested by the last hemistich in 10,17,2, furthermore, the underlying story may also have touched upon the abandonment of the Aśvins, who, although recognized as the true sons of Uṣas and Dyaus, did not fit into the framework of legal marriage.

---

156 Insistence on the virginity of the bride in Vedic society is implicit in the Rigvedic "Wedding hymn" (10,85), especially in a passage most likely alluding to the defloration of the bride (28-30).

This pattern recalls some of the Greek myths treated above, typically involved with bestial rape and the abandonment of heroic offspring. It would thus conform to an already familiar, quasi-universal *modus operandi*. It is significant that Helen was associated with a similar theme in the story, told by Pausanias in *Description of Greece* 2,22,6, of her secretly giving birth to Iphigenia and then assigning the custody of the child to Clytemnestra. We are reminded again of the Thetis/Peleus story, in which Zeus forces Thetis to marry a mortal since she has avoided marriage with him (the version ascribed to Hesiod and the author of the *Cypria*) or because the union of Zeus and Thetis is assumed to result in a son who will be superior to his father. The theriomorphic transformation of Thetis is suggestive in this connection, although the once tempted Zeus is not depicted as perpetrator in this scene.

Suggestive as such patterns may seem, the primary task of the following discussion is not so much to highlight generalities as to discuss some particular traits in the Vedic story that seem uniquely associated with the myth of Helen and the Dioscuri.

### *Helen and Saraṇyū, εἴδωλον and sávarṇa-*

Since we have good reasons to assume connections between the stories of Heaven's incest and the wedding of Saraṇyū, it is motivated to pay further attention to a curious parallel in the myths of Helen and Saraṇyū first noticed by Vittore Pisani.[157] He compared the story of Saraṇyū and her *sávarṇa-* with the story of Helen and her phantom, which is first attested with certainty in Stesichorus' *Palinode* (PMG, 192). According to this early, apparently non-epic Greek tra-

[157] First in the article "Elena e εἴδωλον" from 1929. Then in a revised version, published with an appendix, in the book *Lingue e culture* from 1969.

dition, Helen was kidnapped from her original ravisher Paris, who was given a replica of her (an εἴδωλον). Other scholars have returned to this curious theme, supporting or reconsidering Pisani's original assumption that the stories of Helen and Saraṇyū had a common Indo-European background. [158]

The story behind Stesichoros' *Palinode* (lit. "recantation"), as told by Plato in *Phaedrus* 243a, was that Stesichorus had composed an untruthful poem about Helen and that he had been blinded like Homer because of his sin. Unlike Homer, however, he became aware of the reasons for this punishment and immediately composed a new poem. Plato quotes three verses from the *Palinode*: "That story is not true, and you did not go on the well-benched ships and you did not reach the citadel of Troy" (tr. Campbell). He then concludes that Stesichorus regained his sight as a direct consequence of his recantation. Plato elsewhere (*Republic* 9.586c) explicitly states that Stesichorus had composed a poem about Helen's εἴδωλον, over which the warriors at Troy had fought in ignorance of the truth. Other secondary sources (e.g. Aelius Aristides, *Orationes* 1,128 and P.Oxy. 2506 fr. 26 col. i) suggest that Stesichorus in his poem told about the sea-god Proteus kidnapping Helen from Paris on Pharos (an island west of the Nile delta). According to Euripides (*Helen*) and Herodotus (2,112-120), who were familiar with a similar story, Helen was kept in Egypt during the war, after which she was brought back home to Sparta by Menelaus. Despite the fact that this tradition has not left any clear trace in early epic poetry (the only example is the isolated statement [in Paraphrasis Lycophr. 822] that Helen's phantom was first mentioned by Hesiod [Merkelbach/West, Fr. 358]), it would be naive to assume that Stesichorus invented it *ex nihilo*. It is more likely that Stesichorus was familiar with different versions of Helen's myth, handed down by earlier poets, one of which (by contrast with

---

[158] Notably Christiano Grottanelli (1986) and Otto Skutsch (1987).

the version favored by the Homeric poets) maintained that Helen was robbed from Paris by Proteus, the shape-changing "Old Man of the Sea" referred to in *Od.* 4,349-570, who deluded Paris by creating the εἴδωλον in her place. According to Euripides (*Helen* 31), it was Hera who fashioned Helen's phantom out of compassion for her. In the version related in Euripides and Herodotus, on the other hand, the role of Proteus was that of a righteous king who kept Helen at his court for the sake of her own safety. It is likely, however, that Stesichorus told a slightly different version of the story.

It is quite surprising to find examples, both in Greek and Vedic mythology, of a goddess (or heroine) closely associated with the Dioscuri (or the sons of Dyaus) who is replaced by a replica as a means to delude a mortal husband or ravisher. At the same time we cannot help noticing some apparent differences, such as the fact that Helen is the sister and Saraṇyū the mother of the Dioscuri. An important counterpoise to these differences is the possibility that the names of the two females could reflect a common prototype. This was suggested by Pisani and before him by J. Ehni in 1890.[159] Despite some crucial details of which Pisani could not have been aware, his equation from 1928 still appears perfectly sound. He proceeded from the Proto-Indo-European verbal root **sel*[160] ("to let lose, jump") underlying Vedic √*SAR*, and analyzed the two names as denominatives. From the point of view of contemporary Indo-European linguistics, the name Ἑλένη would then reflect an adjective **sel-en-eh*$_2$ (the same formation, without the feminine suffix *-eh*$_2$, is also seen in Vedic *[su]saraṇá-*) and *Saraṇyū* a Pre-Proto-Indo-Iranian innovation **sel-en-i̯uh*$_2$.

Yet early renderings of the name in two Doric inscription as well as in some less reliable literary sources make this equation problematic. If taken as a whole this evidence clearly indicates that there

---

[159] Skutsch 1987: 190.

[160] Mayrhofer *et al.* suggest **sal* (EWAia, s.v. *SAR*), but see LIV, s.v. 1.**sel*.

was an early tradition of writing Helen's name with initial digamma. Decisive in this regard are two Seventh and Sixth century inscribed bronzes (an aryballos and a meat-hook [?]) from Sparta, found during excavations of the Menelaion in 1975. While the inscription on the aryballos is severely damaged, it can easily be understood with reference to the somewhat younger, undamaged inscription on the meat-hook, which should be read as a dedication: Tᾶι Ϝελέναι "to Welenā."[161] The archaeological context of the two bronzes leaves little doubt that this figure was considered compatible with Homer's Helen. Although the original form of the name is still open to debate, the hypothetical existence of a name beginning with **sel-* (> ἑλ-) could only be adduced with reference to some kind of variation or interference in the treatment and reception of Homer's Helen and the goddess identified with her in Sparta. Such attempts have already been made, and I shall argue here that Pisani's equation still holds on the assumption that a more complex development is assumed.

There is early evidence to suggest that the rendering of Helen's name with initial *h-* did not reflect a form that lost digamma at an early stage, but rather a form beginning with **s-* (which yielded *h-*) that coexisted with a form beginning with **sw-* (which yielded *w-*). This sollution had in fact been suggested by M. Doria before the discovery of the bronzes from Sparta. Two examples are the absence of digamma (in Helen's name) in an early inscription from Tarquina, where two names seem to be given as Ϝλεμαb[α] and Hελε[να], and in the Doric dialect of Corinth (e.g. on two craters from the beginning of the Sixth century), where the letter did not start to disappear until the early Fifth century. Homeric language could of course have had an influence on the spelling of Helen's name, but the same dialect appears less receptive in this regard (as shown in the form *Olysseus* for *Odysseus* on a vase from c.560).[162] Furthermore, there are no traces

---

[161] Catlin/Cavanagh 1976: 153.

[162] Skutsch 1987: 190.

of digamma in the Homeric rendering of Helen's name (although this does not prove the lack of original digamma), and Aeschylus was evidently not familiar with this form despite the Doric stamp of his choruses. A striking example is the chorus' "etymological" play on words in *Agamemnon* 687: Ἑλέναν; ἐπεὶ πρεπόντως ἑλέναυς ἕλανδρος ἑλέπτολις.[163] This alliterative pattern would never apply to certain dialects outside Attica if ϝελένα was unambiguously the recollected Doric name of Homer's Helen, because the suppletive aorist stem ἑλ- (cf. ἑλεῖν as the aor. inf. of αἱρέω "overpower, kill") had no original digamma.

The two solutions to this problem would either be to assume the co-existence and subsequent convergence of two distinct names (with and without initial digamma),[164] or to assume that the two names were simply variants of the same name by reference to the familiar alternation **se-/*su̯e-* (e.g. the numeral **seks/*su̯eks* and the reflexive pronoun **se-, *so-/*su̯e-, *su̯o-*).[165] The former solution appears more attractive in this connection, because a form with initial digamma could be the reflex of another quite accurate characterization of a "Dawn-goddess," derived from the root **su̯el* "to smoulder, burn" (cf. Lith. *svelù* "to glimmer, smoulder," OHG *swellen* "to burn"): **su̯eleneh₂* "the smouldering one." A similar sense is suggested by the noun ἑλένη (or ἑλάνη) meaning "torch" or "corposant." If we assume the parallel existence of two closely associated epithets **su̯eleneh₂* and **seleneh₂*, it is easy to imagine how these eventually got confused in some Greek dialects as a consequence of the loss of digamma. Skutsch took **su̯eleneh₂* and **seleneh₂* to be the names of two different divinities, who "invaded each other's fields and functions."[166] It seems even more compelling to think of

---

[163] See discussion in Schweizer-Keller 1972: 60.

[164] Skutsch 1987: 193.

[165] Oettinger 1999: 263.

[166] Skutsch 1987: 193.

them in terms of different epithets of one and the same figure. Furthermore, the unisonant character of the epithets indicates that they once belonged to the same poetic tradition, evoking a goddess who was mutually "hasty" and "smouldering." Needless to say, others have attempted to etymologize the name of Helen differently. The most recent etymology is found in an article by Stephanie Jamison (Jamison 2001). She proceds from Helen's choice of husband, as characterized by Euripides (*Iph. Aul.* 70-71) (ἣ δ’ εἵλεθ’ [...] Μενέλαον "she chosed [...] Menelaus"), and the Vedic characterization of Sūryā's *svayaṃvara* (or "self-choice") of one out of many suitors. While the root *u̯elh$_1$ is also seen in the term *svayaṃvara*, the comparison would suggest the rendering of Helen's name as *u̯elh$_1$enah$_2$, the "one who choses" (i.e. a husband by her own choice). Jamison's new etymology is also supported by Michael Janda in a recent study (Janda 2005).[167] Although the argument is undoubtedly attractive, it does not strike me as irrefutable.

Pisani identified the reconstructed name *seleneh$_2$ as an epithet of the Indo-European Dawn-goddes (*h$_2$eu̯sōs) by emphasizing the fact that the light of dawn *disappears* as the sun rises. He also stressed that a more precise genealogical connection between this figure and the Divine Twins is unnecessary, since we would be dealing with the personification, or apotheosis, of natural phenomena. As I have demonstrated above with special regard to the Vedic data, the preferable solution to such problems of appellation and genealogy lies rather in the wording and inner logic of the myths themselves. Uṣas could in fact be both sister and mother of the Dioscuri since she was the victim of incest. It is conceivable that such a tradition was decoded differently in different cultural settings. In one of these settings the siblingship was brought out with insistence on the fact that all three (Helen and the Dioscuri) could be identified as the

---

[167] Janda 2005: 346-348.

children of Zeus. In yet another setting the maternity was brought out with less insistence on the siblingship (Saraṇyū). Such genealogical decodings could take place without the underlying effect of some oblique family relations, as indicated by the gradual transfer of characteristics from the Arcadian Pan to the god subsequently regarded as the father of Pan, the once ithyphallic-apotropaic "lesser divinity" Hermes.[168] In the case of Helen and Saraṇyū, however, the apparent dislocation of their family connections could be explained as a segmentation of three original genealogical characteristics, that of sister, daughter, and mother.

A common reference point in both traditions, less pronounced but nevertheless demonstrable in the Greek, is a figure that inherited the name and at least some attributes of the Indo-European Dawn-goddess (**h$_2$eu̯sōs*). Her association with the verbal root **sel* in a more or less specific mythical setting could have passed through different (yet partly overlapping) stages of interpretation (see Fig. 1). By considering the succession of events in the story of Zeus' desire for Nemesis/Leda and the subsequent birth of Helen and the Dioscuri, adding to this story the abduction of Helen and the fashioning of the εἴδωλον, it is easy to notice strong similarities in the Vedic stories of Heaven's incest and the wedding of Saraṇyū. Such similarities could of course be studied synchronically, without regard to any putative common background. Yet if the diachronic dimension is taken into consideration, the partial transparence of the *dramatis personae* clearly indicates that some traits in these traditions (as handed down by Hellenic and Vedic tribes from prehistoric times onwards) belonged to a shared heritage: the Indo-European Sky-god (**di̯ḗu̯s*); the goddess of dawn (**h$_2$eu̯sṓs*), daughter of **di̯ḗu̯s* (**diu̯ós dhugh$_2$tér*); the sons and/or grandsons of **di̯ḗu̯s* (**diu̯ós suHnū́* or **diu̯ós népoth$_1$e*). Other features that recur in both traditions are the fashion-

[168] Cf. Watkins 1970 and Oettinger 1998.

ing of a phantom or replica as a substitute for a ravished or married girl, the Sky-god's metamorphosis and "bestial rape," and possibly the verbal root **sel* ("to let lose, jump") as a typical marker of the daughter/sister and/or the vicitm of rape. The relationship between the mythical agents Dyaus, Uṣas, Saraṇyū, and the Aśvins conforms to a similar logic of combination as does the relationship between Zeus, Helen, and the Dioscuri. Eos could no longer be taken as the daughter of Zeus, nor as the victim of incest or bestial rape, yet she does co-occur with both Helen and the Dioscuri in certain contexts (see Fig. 2 and 3). Whereas the incestuous union between father and daughter is conspicuous in the Vedic sources, such a motif has not left any clear trace in the stories of Zeus and Helen. If, on the other hand, we accept the idea that the Indo-European story of Heaven's incest could appear separately and in a completely different setting as it evolved within Greek tradition, a possible interpretation of this motif can be seen in Orphic renderings of the myth of Zeus and his daughter Persephone. As reported by Athenagoras, one of the early Christian apologists, Zeus was held to have raped his own daughter (herself the outcome of the incestuous union between Zeus and his mother Rhea) "in the form of a snake" (δράκοντος σχήματι). She then gave birth to Dionysos, whose name simply meant "son of Zeus"[169] (*Pro Christian.* 20, Kerns, 58). Once more, just as in the case of Dyaus/Prajāpati in the later versions of the Vedic story, Zeus is transformed into an animal. Even if Miachael Janda may not be wholly justified when assuming that Persephone inherited some salient features from the Indo-European Dawn-goddess,[170] it seems possible to regard this Orphic tradition as another reflex of the (the-

169 This was first suggested by Szemerényi (1971: 665), who argued that "the historical form arose by metathesis (from *ΔιϝοσσυνοϚ) to in ΔιϝοννυσυϚ in which *u-u* was dissimilated to *u-o* as in νυόϚ from **snusus*, ὑιόϚ from ὑιύϚ."

170 See the exhaustive discussion in Janda 2000: 141-176. The still unpublished, but highly convincing, etymology of Persephone's name proposed by Rudolf

riomorhic) union between the Indo-European Sky-god and his own daughter.

As demonstrated above, the application of diachronic perspectives in the study of myth does not imply the search for identical narratives in different traditions. It is rather a matter of treating differences in once more interdependent traditions as the result of reinterpretation and gradual change. An absolute condition in pursuing such a study is that some formal traits in the traditions in question have survived this process of change. Since the technical mode of encoding a message in a poetic or ritual context may be given precedence to the semantic value of the message, a higher degree of persistency is to be expected with regard to formal traits than to those of everyday discourse.

In an attempt to substantiate the assumption that the story of Helen and the birth of the Dioscuri in fact developed from an Indo-European plot, parts of which eventually became favorite foci of epic song, this discussion now turns to a theme associated with the subsequent career of the Dioscuri.

---

Wachter (**persó-* + **$g^{wh}$en* "beating the sheaves") makes any association with a Dawn-goddess seem less convincing.

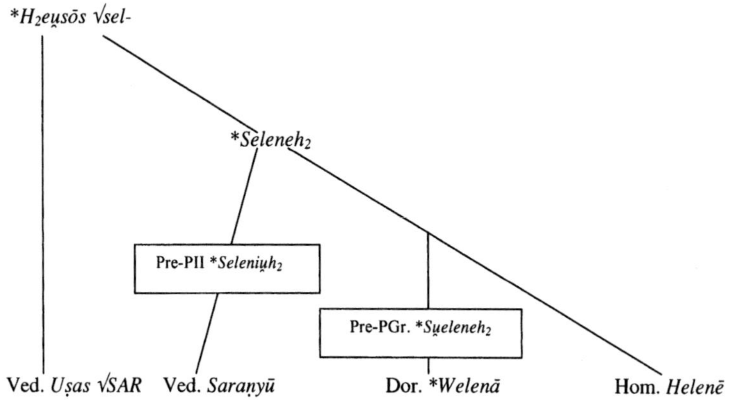

Fig. 1

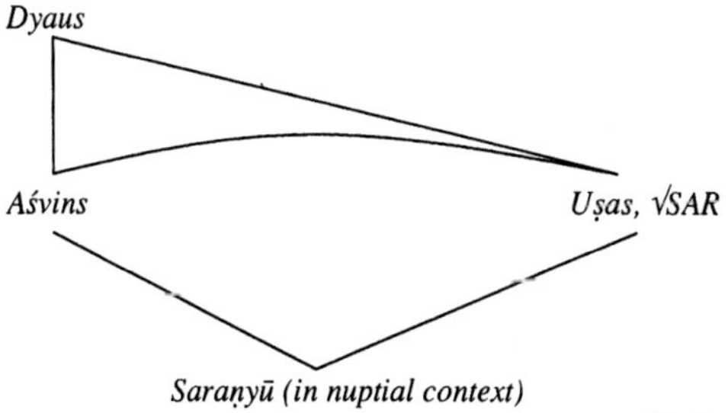

Fig. 2

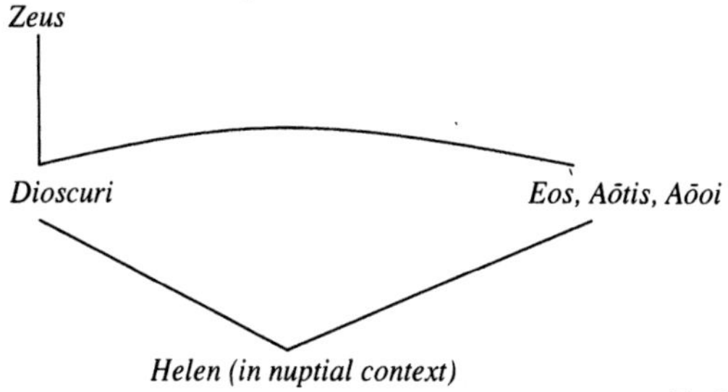

Fig. 3

# III.
# RETURNING HEROES

In the epic tradition, a song about the return of Achaean heroes from Troy was referred to as a Νόστος (or in the plural Νόστοι, henceforth [as regards the generic label] *Nostos, Nostoi*). Although the primary sense of this term was simply "return (home)," its etymology and specific employment within the genre itself was underpinned by a rather complex set of notions. The pre-existence of such a genre at the earliest stage of Homeric composition is strongly suggested by the description of the singer Phemius in the first book of the *Odyssey*, who sings of "the return of the Achaeans" (Ἀχαιῶν νόστον, 1,326) in the palace of the absent king at Ithaca. Early examples of poets working within this tradition are Eumelos of Corinth, who is said to have composed a νόστος τῶν Ἑλλήνων (Schol. Pind. Ol. 13,31), an unnamed Colophonian poet mentioned by Lysimachos (Eustathius 1796, 45), and Stesichorus (who, in his *Nostoi*, also must have included the story of Odysseus [PMG, 208, 209]). During the late Hellenistic period, a *Nostoi* consisting of five books was attributed to the poet Agias of Troizen, and it is to this work that Proclus refers in his summary of the Trojan Cycle (*Chrestomathia,* suppleta ex Apollod. epit. 6.1-30).

Despite the apparent fact that the actual, fixed poems referred to as "Nostoi" by ancient authors were more or less dependent on the *Odyssey* (the description of *other* returns than *the* return of Homer's Odysseus), there is no doubt that the *Odyssey* emerged from a well-established tradition. Examples of images from the Archaic Age about the return of the Greeks from Troy (referred to by Burgess as *Returns* without reference to the Epic Cycle), which do not seem to be based on any specific poem, are listed in an appendix (C) to Burgess' book.[171] It is conceivable, furthermore, that the generic label itself belonged to this tradition, just as did the "fame of men" (κλέα ἀνδρῶν) sung by the blind singer Demodocus at the Phaeacians' feast (*Od.* 8,73). It is the purpose of this chapter to look for concepts and motifs that could have triggered the formation of such a genre. In doing so, however, the discussion does not restrict itself to the *Nostos* as a part of anything specifically "Trojan." The point that I make here, which of course has to remain purely hypothetical, is rather that the story of a hero's return as elaborated in the *Odyssey* (and possibly in poems of a much earlier date) conformed to a pattern that also involved events discussed in the previous chapter: the conception and birth of the Dioscuri (or Divine Twins), Helen as an instrument in the execution of the Διὸς βουλή, and the safe return of a devout mortal as a result of divine intervention.

## *Nestor, *nes, and the Nāsatyas*

In a forthcoming study, Douglas Frame sheds new light on the origin of Nestor by developing ideas already introduced in his book *The Myth of Return in Early Greek Epic*. In his first book, Frame offered a new analysis of the root **nes* (Gr. νόστος, νέομαι, ἄσμενος, etc.), which he understood as a formal and semantic equivalent of Gr. νόος (meaning "mind, perception"). The form underlying νόος would thus be **nosos*, related to the verb νέομαι as λόγος is to λέγω and φόβος to φέβομαι. On the basis of Myceanean evidence (e.g. the proper noun *wi-pi-no-o-* [= Gr. Ἰφίνοος] and the treatment of Greek -νόος in compounds), Frame suggested that earlier etymologies should be abandoned (forms with intervocalic digamma or initial *s*-).[172] He found convincing evidence for a semantic rationale of

[171] Burgess 2001: 36,186f.

[172] Frame 1978: 2ff.

νόστος and νόοος in the story of Odysseus and his "foolish" companions, which seems to explore the idea that the companions lost their return (νόστος) for lack of intelligence (νόος), whereas Odysseus embodies the intelligence that saves him from death and brings about his safe return.[173] Frame also turned to other Indo-European traditions in order to show that the root **nes* in fact conveyed the complex notion "bring back to life and light (from death and darkness)," which could apply to the diurnal and nocturnal journey(s) of the sun. Furthermore, he regarded the activities and verbal tags of the Aśvins (or Nāsatyas) in Vedic mythology as important clues to his hypothesis.[174] Such allegorical interpretations of the *Odyssey* may conform to its reception as a work of art,[175] but they do not necessarily constitute its foundation. Although I see no obvious reason to read the *Odyssey* as a "solar myth," I would still support the "early" Frame in regarding the root **nes* as a major clue to the Indo-European background of the story. This point becomes even more compelling in the new analysis of the name and function of Nestor in the *Odyssey*. Among the numerous reasons for regarding Nestor as a key-figure in the story (all of which are carefully presented in Frame's forthcoming book), I will merely focus biefly on the meaning of Nestor's name, his association with the Indo-European Divine Twins, and with the Phaeacian king Alcinoos.

It has often been noticed that the name Nestor could be taken as an agent noun with the root **nes* (as in νέομαι) and the suffix *-tor*. While the meaning of the name has usually been understood in the intransitive sense (cf. Frisk "der [glücklich wohin] gelangt," s.v. νέομαι) with reference to the meaning of the middle verb νέομαι "to return," Frame shows that the name is best understood in the

[173] Frame 1978: ch. 3 (pp. 34-80).

[174] Frame 1978: ch. 6 (pp. 125-152).

[175] This view clearly gained popularity during later phases, notably in Parmienides and Plotinus. Cf. Mourelatos 1970: 32ff.

transitive sense as "he who brings back." This new interpretation of the name is supported by the meaning of the name of Nestor's father, Neleus, which, with reference to earlier and similar forms attested in Greek (such as Αγέλαως, Myc. Gr. **Nehelawos*, and Myc. Gr. **Arkhelawos*), could only be understood in the transitive sense as "he who leads the warfolk home" (with the active verb *νέ[σ]ω "bring back").[176]

Nestor's association with the Divine Twins as they appear in Vedic mythology is not only immediately given on a formal level—their chief epithet (*nā́sasatya-*) evidently contains the root **nes*—it could also be further elaborated with reference to Nestor's myth in Greek epic and to his epithet "horseman" (ἵπποτα). By following Stig Wikander, according to whom the treatment of the Aśvins (or their epic avatars Nakula and Sahadeva) in Sanskrit epic tradition clearly shows that one of the twins was considered "warlike" and the other characterized as being "intelligent,"[177] Frame suggests that the "horseman Nestor" could be regarded as a twin figure, who incorporated the features of his "warlike" (mortal) brother Periclymenos, thus taking over his original epithet ἵπποτα. Seeing that the epithet ἵπποτα contains the same Indo-European element (*$h_1$*eḱu̯o-* "horse") as the one retained in the Vedic adjective *aśvín-* ("horseman, possessing horses"), it is conceivable that the two epithets originally pertained to each twin individually. Others have already argued that the Vedic epithets were used as elliptical duals in the earliest texts, and that one of the twins was originally referred to as *aśvín-*, while the other was referred to as *nā́satya*.[178] Frame also highlights this

[176] See Frame (forthcoming).

[177] Wikander 1957.

[178] Cf. Mayrhofer's reference to T. Gotō in EWAia, s.v. *nā́satya-*. Such elliptic tendencies are also seen in the parallel employment of the epithets "Dioscuri" and "Tyndaraidae," as exemplified by the longer *Homeric Hymn to the Dioscuri* (1-2).

possibility by quoting a passage in the Rigveda (2,41,7) where the duals are clearly contrasted, as if intended to emphasize the twins' individual characteristics.

In the genealogies of Nestor and another key-figure in the *Odyssey*, Alcinoos, the myth of the Divine Twins once more surfaces. Both Nestor and Alcinoos have "warlike" (mortal) brothers (Periclymenos and Rhexenor). They both descend from founders of a new city, Neleus and Nausithoos, who in their turn descend from Poseidon and the sole surviving daughters (Tyro and Pariboia) of kings (Salmoneus and Eurymedon). Furthermore, the name of Alcinoos most likely contains the root **nes*, and Frame takes it to mean "he who brings back (**nosos*) by his strength (ἀλκί, the heteroclitic [instrumental] dative of ἀλκή)." Adding to this interpretation of Alcinoos' name, I would suggest as curiosity, a possible confluence of these two aspects occurs in a Vedic characterization of the two Aśvins: the "strength/protection" (Gr. ἀλκή/ἀλέξω, Vedic √*RAKṢ* < **$h_2$elk, *$h_2$leks* "to hold back, protect") and the capacity to "bring home" (**nes*). It is seen in the following hemistich (RV 2,39,6c): *nā́seva nas tanvò rakṣitā́rā* "as the nose (be, you Aśvins/Nāsatyas) the protectors of our body." Since the simile appears somewhat farfetched at a first glance (the nose as the protector of the body), we must assume that the poet also intended *nā́seva nas* to serve as a verbal echo of the name of the gods (*nā́satya-*) to which the entire hymn was addressed. The twins would then be characterized as the *rakṣitā́rā* of the body in their capacity as "bringing home," thus uniting the two qualities reflected by the name of Alcinoos.

While these issues are analyzed in much more detail by Frame, I will content myself with observing (following Frame) that Nestor and Alcinoos, the two figures more or less explicitly functioning as Odysseus' rescuers, apparently convey features that were already associated with the Divine Twins in Vedic mythology. It is difficult to answer why and how the Phaeacians entered into this framework.

Suffice it to say that their story seems uniquely associated with the *Odyssey*,[179] suggesting that its putative background, if at all important to other poets, may have had a different outcome in other renderings of the same hereditary subject-matter. Furthermore, their role in the *Odyssey* (especially as manifested in descriptions of their former homeland Hyperia) evokes aspects elsewhere associated with Aphrodite and Eos. This point supports Boedeker's assumption that the Divine Twins, in their role as allies of the Dawn-goddess, travelling from the matutinal regions in the East, were possible prototypes of the Phaeacians.[180]

Before once more turning to the Vedic material, we should also consider to what extent the Dioscuri proper could function as rescuers at sea in early Greek literature.

## *The Dioscuri as Rescuers at Sea*

The specific sense of the Dioscuric epithet σωτῆρες "saviours," which is attested as early as Terpander (PMG, 4), is foregrounded in the longer *Homeric Hymn to the Dioscuri* (no. 33 in Allen's edition). Early characterizations of the hymn as a late work[181] had to be abandoned when Allen/Halliday/Sikes (in their second edition of *The Homeric Hymns* from 1963) brought attention to a Sixth century bronze disc from Cephalenia, which most likely "quotes" the hymn or an early version of it (ΔιϜὸς κώροιν μεγάλοιο).[182] The leading theme of the hymn is the Dioscuri as saviours of men on sea (6-7).

[179] As noted by Frame in his forthcoming work, this was early suggested by Nitzsch in *Anmerkungen zur Odyssee*, vol. 2, p. 781.

[180] See Boedeker 1974: 53f. and 56f.

[181] E.g. Gemoll 1886: "Die Flügel der Dioskuren (vs. 13) lassen den Hymnus erst auf eine sehr junge Zeit setzen."

[182] Allen/Halliday/Sikes 1963: 441.

When storms rage over the sea, the sailors are said to promise the twins offerings of white lambs (7-10) and when the ship is about to sink the Dioscuri come flying through the air to rescue the shipwrecked sailors. The Dioscuri are "fair signs" (σήματα καλά) who put asunder toil (11-17). As we shall see below, this hymn conveys notions that most likely belonged to the earliest manifestation of the Dioscuri in Greek religion. The twins do not appear in their role as epic characters or (divinized) heroes (which is also suggested by their mere inclusion in this collection), but as saviours of distressed mortals and recipients of animal offerings. It is possible that their active appearance in the world of mortals, along with the notion that one of the twins was a mortal, made it easier to associate them with the heroic plane in epic poetry. However, this by no means proves that their position in early Greek religion was dictated by such epic renderings.

Another early invocation of the Dioscuri as saviours at sea is found in a fragment by Alcaeus (L-P, B2), where the twins are said to go on swift horses on land and sea, rescuing men from death (5-8). They are also said to be "leaping upon the peaks of the well-benched ships" (εὐσ̣δ[ύγ]ων θρῴσκοντ̣[ες ἐπ'] ἄκρα νάων [9]), an image that many commentators interpret as a reference to the phenomenon known as St. Elmos fire: an electrical discharge creating a glow about the mast-head and rigging of ships.[183] In this capacity, they are "bringing light to the ships in a grievous night" (ἀργαλέᾳ δ' ἐν νύκτι φ[άος φέ]ροντες νᾶϊ [11-12]).

A third example, possibly more dependent on epic imagery but nevertheless significant in this connection, is an allusion to Helen's own *Nostos* in Euripides' *Helen* (1642ff.). Towards the end of the play, the Dioscuri appear in the air above the stage to prevent Theoclymenos (the brother of the dead king Proteus) from killing his own

---

[183] See, for instance, Campbell 1982: 247.

sister Theoone (who has betrayed him by helping Helen to escape from Egypt with Menelaus). It was the gods' wish that Helen should return home and reunite with Menelaos. The Dioscuri then address Helen, who has begun her journey with Menelaus back to Sparta, assuring her that they, her "saviours" (σωτῆρε [1664]), her "two brothers riding the sea" (κασιγνήτω διπλὼ πόντον παριππεύοντε [1664-5]), "shall lead her back to her native country" (πέμψομεν πάτραν [1665]). That the similar expression πεμπ- ἐς πατρίδα was already formulaic in Homer is clearly indicated by different passages alluding to the attempted or successful return of Achaean heroes as the result of divine or semi-divine intervention (*Od.* 4,586 [of Menelaus assisted by "immortals"], 5,37 [of Odysseus assisted by the Phaeaceans], 13,53 [of Odysseus assisted by the Phaeaceans], 14,333 [of Odysseus], 19,290 [of Odysseus], 23,315 [of Odysseus assisted by Aeolus], 23,340 [of Odysseus assisted by the Phaeacieans]).

As noticed by Richard Kannicht (432), this particular passage in Euripides' play contains the direct response to a prayer addressed to the Dioscuri by the chorus, embedded in the so called "Propemptikon" (a poetically designed prayer for a "fair voyage" [εὔπλοια]) in a previous section of the drama (1451-1511 [1495-1505]).[184] Prayers belonging to this genre, sometimes explicitly addressing the Dioscuri, have been found in inscriptions from the harbour of Prote (IG V1, 1548-41) and in a badly damaged inscription from Attica (IG I² 127). The inscription from Attica even suggests that the festival of the Dioscuri in Athens, the so called Ἀνάκεια, was particularly devoted to the Ἄνακε (an old epithet of the Dioscuri) as gods of sailors. We may thus assume that the Propemptikon in *Helen*, as well as the *Homeric Hymn to the Dioscuri* and the fragment by Alcaeus (L-P, 34), were all modelled upon an old supplicatory genre particularly favoured by Greek seamen.[185]

---

[184] Kannicht 1969: 432.

[185] See discussion in Kannicht 1969: 374, 392.

As it seems, the role of the Dioscuri in Euripides' *Helen* is mutually connected with the actual context of their worship in Greek religion and epic renderings of a hero's return in the Cyclic tradition. In this regard, therefore, Euripides' drama provides a link between the sphere of ritual, in which the Dioscuri were treated as equals of the other Greek gods, and the epic sphere, in which they chiefly belonged to the heroic plane. If the epic treatment of a hero's *Nostos* also had its equivalence in a liturgical context, it would be fully consistent to associate the Dioscuri with this motif. Such a liturgical context is by necessity implicit in all of the Vedic hymns, and by considering their treatment of the Aśvins (or Nāsatyas) as rescuers at sea we will recognize aspects of these figures that were less pronounced in Greek epic. It is my assumption that these facts about the Aśvins and the Dioscuri describe the contours of the same narrative tradition.

### *The Story of Bhujyu and Indo-Iranian Rescue epyllia*

There is a curious Vedic genre of rescue *epyllia* (or micro-*epyllia*) either involving the two Aśvins, or the god Indra. While these stories are often only briefly hinted at, they all conform to a similar pattern: a devout mortal has been abandoned at a distant or desolate place and/or is tormented by hostile beings, but the gods (or the god) suddenly come to his rescue, either healing him or bringing him back home. As for the Aśvins, allusions to such *epyllia* are particularly salient in a group of hymns found in the first Maṇḍala (112-121). Another implicit reference to the genre is found in one of the hymns ascribed to the poet Dīrghatamas (RV 1,158). The hymn contains allusions to a legend associated with the poet himself, in which he was addressing the Aśvins in distress (at sea?) by simultaneously alluding to situations similar to that of his own. One such "situation" is encoded in the story of Traitana, a heroic figure who rescues a mortal (Rebha or other) floating fesseled at sea by killing one or several hostile beings referred to as *dāsá-*. Another legend involves the mortal Bhujyu, who was left at sea by his father Tugra and eventually brought back home by the Aśvins.

This singular reference to the story of Traitana in the Rigveda has apparently been misunderstood by most scholars and indigenuous commentators. It was only recently that Traitana could be demonstrated to be both formally and functionally identical with the Iranian hero Θraēta(o)na, who likewise rescues a devout mortal at sea (the *vifra-* [cf. Vedic *vípra-* "singer, poet"] Pāuruua [cf. Vedic Paura]), kills a Dāsa [cf. Avestan Dahāka], and brings the mortal back home [Yašt 5,61ff.]).[186] The reconsideration of this passage has important implications for the general problems addressed in this chapter, because it gives us reason to believe that the rescue *epyllia* alluded to in the Vedic hymns in fact belonged to a genre that was already fully developed at the time of Indo-Iranian unity.

The story of Bhujyu, which is also alluded to by Dīrghatamas (1,158,3), is specifically associated with the Aśvins. Allusions to the same story are found in at least fifteen other Rigvedic hymns, some of which devote more than one stanza to it (1,112,6.20; 1,116,3-5; 1,117,14-15; 1,119,4.8; 1,182,5-7). This is a significant number, since many allusions to other (presumably similar) "stories" basically consist of mentioning only the name of the mortal involved. Regarding the story of Bhujyu, consider, for instance, the following passage (1,116,3-5):

3. túgro ha bhujyúm aśvinodameghé ˈ rayíṃ ná káś cin mamr̥vā́ṁ ávāhāḥ | tám ūhatur naubhír ātmanvátībhir ˈ antarikṣaprúdbhir ápodakābhiḥ || 4. tisráḥ kṣápas trír áhātivrájadbhir ˈ nā́satyā bhujyúm ūhathuḥ pataṃgaíḥ ||

---

[186] For a detailed analysis of the comparative evidence, see Jackson/Oettinger 2002.

samudrásya dhánvan ārdrásya pāré ' tribhī́ ráthaiḥ śatápadbhiḥ ṣá̱laśvaiḥ || 5. anārambhaṇé tád avīrayethām ' anāsthāné agrabhaṇé samudré | yád aśvinā ūhátur bhujyúm ástam ' śatā́ritrāṃ nā́vam ātasthivā́ṃsam ||

"3. Verily, Tugra had left Bhujyu behind in the "watery cloud" (= the sea?), o Aśvins, just as any of those who are dead (has left behind) his property. Him you two carried with animated ships, floating in the air, waterless. 4. For three nights, and with wings going across (a space of) three times days, you Nāsatyas carried Bhujyu on to the shore of the sea, on to the farther border of the moistness, with three hundred-footed, six-horsed chariots. 5. In the sea, without anything to hold on to, without standpoint, without handle, you two proved to be heroes, when you Aśvins carried Bhujyu home, he who embarked on (your) hundred-oared ship."

Certain details stand out as particularly relevant to the appreciation of the passage in a larger context, because they seem to constitute unique realizations of the story as it is alluded to elsewhere in the Rigveda: 1) the characterization of the ships in which the Aśvins carry Bhujyu back home, i.e. the fact that the ships have souls or selves (*ātmán*), that they are animated or automated (*ātmanvát*), and 2) the expression signaling the fact that Bhujyu was "carried home" (*√VAH ástam*).

To the best of my knowledge, the notion of an animated ship or boat is only attested once elsewhere in the Rigveda, significantly in a stanza referring to the craft that carried Bhujyu home (*plávam ātmanavantam* "animated boat," 1,182,5ab). There are some references to "self-harnessing" (*sváyukta-, sváyukti-*) vehicles or draught-animals, such as the chariot of the Sun-god Sūrya (1,50,9), but this adjective could also be associated with the return of Bhujyu (*yuvám bhujyúm bhurámāṇam víbhir gatáṃ ' sváyuktibhir niváhantā pitṛ́bhya ā́* "you two, coming to the quivering Bhujyu with self-harnessing birds, carrying him home [*ni+√VAH*] to his two parents[187],"

[187] Cf. πάτρα, the word for "native country" or "fatherland" (especially in the expression πέμψομεν πάτραν [see above]), which reflects the same Indo-Eu-

1,119,4ab). This rarely attested notion regarding the miraculous vehicles of the Aśvins seems to match a similarly isolated notion, attested only once in the *Odyssey* (8,555-63), regarding the Phaeacean ships that eventually carry Odysseus back home:

> εἰπὲ δέ μοι γαῖάν τε τεὴν δῆμόν τε πόλιν τε,
> ὄφρα σε τῇ πέμπωσι τιτυσκόμενοι φρεσὶ νῆες·
> οὐ γὰρ Φαιήκεσσι κυβερνητῆρες ἔασιν,
> οὐδέ τι πηδαλι' ἔστι, τά ἄλλαι νῆες ἔχουσιν·
> ἀλλ' αὐταὶ ἴσσασι πόλιας καὶ πίονας ἀγροὺς
> ἀνθρώπων, καὶ λαῖτμα τάχισθ' ἁλὸς ἐκπερόωσιν
> ἠέρι καὶ νεφέλῃ κεκαλυμμέναι· οὐδέ ποτέ σφιν
> οὔτε τι πημανθῆναι ἔπι δέος οὔτ' ἀπολέσθαι.

"Tell me your land, your neighborhood and your city, so that our ships, straining with their own purpose (τιτυσκόμενοι φρεσὶ νῆες), can carry you there, for there are no steersmen among the Phaiakians, neither are there any steering oars for them, such as other ships have, but the ships themselves understand men's thoughts and purposes, and they know all the cities of men and all their fertile fields, and with greatest speed they cross the gulf of the salt sea, huddled under a mist and cloud, nor is there ever any fear that they may suffer damage or come to destruction. " (Tr. Richmond Lattimore)

Even though direct etymological connections between the linguistic characterization of the ships of the Aśvins and those of the Phaeaceans are missing (with the exception of the commonplace word for "ship" [Vedic *náu-*, Hom. ναῦς]), the notion as such is so specific that its employment in this particular context does not seem purely accidental. This is particularly noteworthy since the Phaeaceans could be demonstrated to have borrowed certain features from the Greek Dioscuric tradition (as suggested by the name, story, and genealogy of Alcinoos as well as epic references to the original homeland of the Phaeaceans in Hyperia). It should not be ruled out

---

ropean noun as the Vedic dual *pitṝ́bhya.*

that both comparanda vaguely reflect a play on words that once involved the unisonant components **nostos, *nosos, *nes, *naus,* etc., to which we may also add Alcaeus' possible characterization of the Dioscuri as having an εὔνοος θυμός "well-disposed mind" (see the restoration of L-P, B2,3). The deverbative νόημα recurs in another passage characterizing the Phaeacean ships with particular emphasis on their speed, rather than their automated steering. At *Odyssey* 7,36, their ships are said to be swift as a wing or a thought (τῶν νέες ὠκεῖαι ὡς εἰ πτερὸν ἠὲ νόημα). Although this particular simile is more salient in the Rigveda (e.g. the adjective *mánojavas-* "swift as thought") than in Homer, it is still significant that it applies to the miraculous vehicle (this time a chariot) in which Bhujyu was rescued by the Aśvins (*ūhathuḥ* [...] *ráthena ' mánojavasā* "they [the Aśvins] carried him [Taugrya, i.e. the son of Tugra {= Bhujyu}] in a chariot swift as thought," 1,117,15).

As indicated above, the name *nā́satya-* most likely belongs to the verbal root **nes* (Vedic √*NAS*).[188] This interpretation neither raises any serious formal problems, nor does it appear the least problematic in the light of the mythical characterization of these figures (they are indeed depicted as "homebringers" in the Vedic hymns). The long *-ā-* could be explained as a Vr̥ddhi-formation of an unattested noun **nas-atí-* (as in *vas-atí* "[night-)]dwelling"). Although the name has an indisputable Indo-Iranian background (cf. Mittani Aryan *na-ša-at-ti-i̯a-an-na* and the Young Avestan m. sg. *nā̊ŋhaiθiia-*), it is difficult to provide a more detailed characterization of these figures on the basis of non-Vedic evidence.[189] As exemplified by the passage

---

188 Cf. EWAia, s.v. *nā́satya-*.

189 The formulaic coincidence YAv. *iṇdrəm* [...] *nā̊ŋaiθīm daēum* ~ Ved. *índra-nāsatyā* (cf. Mayrhofer EWAia s.v. *nā́satya-* [with references]) indicates that the Indo-Iranian antecedents of *Nā̊ŋhaiθiia/Nā́satya-* (< IIr. **Nā́sati̯a-*) had dealings with the god **Indra-* resembling those to which many of the Vedic hymns subscribe.

quoted from RV 1,116 above, the "homebringing" aspect is in fact further emphasized by the simple formula √*VAH ástam*. It is only attested three times in the Rigveda, and except for the passage already quoted it is once more employed in the context of the distressed Bhujyu (*ástaṃ váyo na túgryam* "as the bird [← carried {√*VAH*}] the son of Tugra *home* [*ástam*]," 8,3,23c). The formation and semantics of this noun are in fact closely related to that of Gr. νόστος. Both forms seem to be substantivizations of the root with different vowel gradations (either **ns-tó-* [as reflected by *ásta-*] or **nos-tó-* [as reflcted by νόστος]). The accent on the first syllable is probably secondary.[190] We could even venture to compare these nouns from the point of view of prosody. Two Vedic stanzas alluding to the story of Bhujyu with the verse-final or half-verse-final employment of the accusative *ástam* (one of which occurs in an apochryphal so-called *Khila*) are reminiscent of the pattern peculiar to the latter half of a paroemiac, which also may include the accusative νόστον (– ⏑ ⏑ – ⏓). Compare the following examples:.

A. bhuj*i*úm ástam (RV 1,116,5c)
B. taugr*i*ám ástam (Khil. 2,1b)
C. mḗdeto nóston (Od. 3,132, 160)
D. -aínuto nóston (Od. 12,419, 14,309)

The identification of some recurrent semantic and formal elements in the realization of Bhujyu's story—the employment of the formula √*VAH ástam* and the closely related notions of animated ships and vehicles "swift as thought"—indicates that the confluence of these (or very similar) elements in the epic rendering of Odysseus' return was in fact engendered by a much older, pre-Homeric tradition involving the Divine Twins as rescuers at sea. The early Greek poets'

---

[190] EWAia, s.v. *ásta-*.

reference to this tradition (and the genre engendered by it) as *Nostoi* is symptomatic in this regard, especially since we can show that a similar concept (*ástam*) was favoured by Vedic poets alluding to stories that also had other features in common with those associated with the major *Nostos* of Greek epic: Homer's *Odyssey*.

# IV.
# EPILOGUE: THE ROOTS OF THE TROJAN CYCLE

The point that I am going to make in this epilogue may seem provocative to some, not least in the absence of a more solid repertoire of evidence and informed reasoning. Yet it should be permissible to raise questions and suggest preliminary solutions if only to see these preliminaries shattered by more convincing suggestions.

My basic questions could be summarized as follows: How did the plot of the "Trojan Cycle" develop? What was the stuff of this plot at the time of pre-Homeric composition? Could anything be said regarding the prehistory of the single motifs and their logic of combination by turning to traditions with which the Greeks shared a common poetic heritage?

These questions could either be refuted on the grounds of being wrongly put or with reference to a lack sufficient evidence for providing any conclusive answers. Assuming that such objections are not necessarily valid in this case, I shall attempt to sketch a possible scenario on the basis of data discussed in the previous chapters. The extreme points of the Trojan Cycle could be fixed to the following events: (1) the design and execution of Zeus' plan (the Διὸς βουλή) through the begetting of Helen and Achilles, the two "instruments" of the plan, and (2) the home-coming and subsequent death of Odysseus, the last Achaean hero to return from Troy. These are the two ends tied together to form the "Trojan Cycle." If we think of the poems traditionally assigned to this cyclic arrangement as a series A → B → C → D → E → F → G → H, the initial event would belong to the fragmented poem *Cypria* (A) and the final events to the *Odyssey* (G) and the likewise fragmented *Telegony* (H). The Trojan War and the devastating "wrath of Akhilles" (B) may be regarded as the climactic fulfillment of the divine plan. While the story of Odysseus belongs to the aftermath of the divine plan, it also describes its inversion and abolition: human design and divine benevolence eventually allowing the hero to escape divine wrath.

What was the original outline of the divine plan and what seems to have been its cause? According to an early scholiastic tradition, Zeus felt pity for the overburdened Earth and wanted to relieve her through a depopulation of mankind. The seven lines quoted from an unknown epic poem often identified as the *Cypria* (although probably from a different poem) in Schol. A. Vind 61 may be considered particularly relevant:

> ἦν ὅτε μυρία φῦλα κατὰ χθόνα πλαζομένα [αἰεί
> ἀνθρώπων ἐ]βαρυ[νε βαθυ]στέρνου πλάτος αἴης,
> Ζεὺς δὲ ἰδὼν ἐλέησε, καὶ ἐν πυκιναῖς πραπίδεσσιν
> κουφίσαι ἀνθρώπων παμβώτορα σύνθετο γαῖαν,
> ῥιπισσας πολέμου μεγάλην ἔριν Ἰλιακοῖο,
> ὄφρα κενώσειεν θανάτου βάρος. οἱ δ' ἐνὶ Τροίηι
> ἥρωες κτείνοντο. Διὸς δ' ἐτελείετο βουλή.

> "There was a time when the countless races [of men] roaming [constantly] over the land were weighing down the [deep-]breasted earth's expanse. Zeus took pity when he saw it, and in his complex mind he resolved to relieve the all-nurturing earth of mankind's weight by fanning the great conflict of the Trojan War, to void the burden through death. So the warriors at Troy kept being killed, and Zeus' plan was fulfilled." (Tr. Martin West)

This and other early commentators (e.g. Eustathius) maintain that the birth of Helen and the marriage of Thetis, rather than the usual cataclysmal characteristics of depopulation, such as lightning or flood, should be the instruments of the plan. Although some of the texts quoted in the scholia need not belong to the earliest strata of epic poetry, there is nothing to suggest that the instrumentality of

Helen and Achilles, as well as the divine plan of depopulation, were *not* themes maintained in the early tradition as well.[191]

Modern scholars have reconsidered the actual reason for depopulation by turning to epic texts less favoured by the scholiasts. One such example is a fragment of the Hesiodic *Catalogue of Women* (Fr. 204MW), according to which Zeus plans to begin the cycle of seasons and separate gods from men.[192] Within this larger scheme, the Trojan War (apart from relieving the overburdened Earth) marks the end of the Golden Age and the beginning of the human condition. Another important clue to this scheme is the marriage of Thetis. According to Laura Slatkin, Zeus gives the desired Thetis to a mortal in order to end the struggle for divine succession. If Zeus should marry Thetis himself, his son would become mightier than him and thus maintain strife among the gods.[193]

Other stories of this kind were familiar to the Greeks, not least the legend of Pyrrha and Deukalion. Such stories may in fact be endemic to mythical thought, because they seem to thematize societal obstacles that could trigger discrete but similar cultural responses.[194] However, my main reason for bringing up the depopulation theme here is not its quasi-universality. Rather, I want to elucidate a generic background of the Trojan Cycle that seems to have underpinned, yet without being easily recognizable in the extant texts, the narratives elaborated in early epic tradition.

Kenneth Mayer has noticed that classical scholars often approach the depopulation theme in Greek mythology as a conflict between different traditions, one of which is usually interpreted as having influenced the other.[195] This assumed priority especially concerns

---

191 Mayer 1996: 2.

192 Reference to Nagy (1979: 220) in Meyer, ibid.

193 Reference to Slatkin (1991: *passim*) in Mayer, ibid.

194 Mayer, ibid: 4.

195 Ibid.

the themes of impure creation (Zeus mating with Nemesis) and divine succession (Zeus suspending his desires to mate with Thetis). According to Mayer, the flawed element of creation and the closure of divine succession should both be understood as integrated parts of Zeus' plan to initiate the human condition and bring misery down to Earth. This pattern, he argues, can also be deduced by comparing the tradition attested in the *Cypria* with similar overpopulation/depopulation myths from the Near East (such as the Babylonian epic *AtraḪasis*), Iran, and India. As indicated above, however, Mayer first of all adheres to the synchronic significance of such parallels. My own perspective differs from Mayer's in that I am not adducing typologies beyond the sphere of historical contingency as my primary source of information. On the other hand, I share his implicit assumption that such typological parallels are never sufficient criteria of a common origin. Instead, I want to consider the possibility that some specific elaborations of this synchronic pattern did in fact evolve, not through the memory of past events, but through the impetus of a shared oral tradition.

Although Indic and Iranian traditions about depopulation show great variation, it is worth noticing that they assign special importance to Yama/Yima and Manu, two affiliated figures belonging to the mythical past. Iranian Yima (cf. Indo-Iranian **[H]i̯ama-*), the son of Vīuuaŋ$^{v}$haṇt (cf. Ved. Vivasvat), is the main character in a story about the end of the Golden Age (first attested in the *Vīdēvdāt* 2,21-43). Furthermore, the Indic progenitor Manu (IIr. **Manu[š]*) is the main character in a story about a great cataclysm (ŚB 1,8,1-10, Mahābhārata [Vanaparvan 12747-12802]). Apart from their mutual appearance in stories about depopulation, both figures are linked to the Rigvedic story of Saraṇyū. According to early renderings, Yama (a first or second generation mortal, conceptualized as a figure of Dẹath in later sources) appears as the only child of Vivasvat and Saraṇyū, whereas Manu is conceived as the child of Vivasvat and

Saraṇyū's "phantom" Sāvarṇī (RV 10,62,11). Yama and Manu would thus represent the most conspicuously mortal outcome of Saraṇyū's dealings, balanced by the divine or semi-divine outcome represented by the Aśvins (the *dívo nápātā*).

If all these facts are brought together and analyzed as a whole, the story of Saraṇyū appears to form a part of a more extensive narrative treatment of mankind as the by-product of impure creation, introducing the notion of a great cataclysm from which only a small portion of the mortal community is saved. In their prominent role as saviours of mortals at sea, the Aśvins would fit well into this narrative plot for purely thematic reasons. More importantly, however, they clearly do belong to the plot in their capacity as sons of Saraṇyū. Despite these clues, the events surrounding the birth of the Aśvins are never presented as a pretext of their future role as saviours at sea, nor do the Vedic homecoming variations (as analyzed above) adhere to a more general cataclysmic plot. It is rather the Greek data that provide a viable interface in this regard.

As demonstrated in the previous chapters, the affiliation of Helen and the Dioscuri in Greek epic and mythography is conspicuous both at the event of their miraculous birth (bestial rape, intervention of mortal lover, divine as well as mortal offspring) and in a typical rescue action, ultimately induced by Zeus' plan to depopulate the Earth (Helen's safe return to Sparta, the "Propemptikon"). In the latter case, we recognize the Dioscuri as Helen's "saviours," as her "two brothers riding the sea" (Eurdipides' *Helen* [1664-5]). We noticed above that Helen was decisive of Zeus' execution of the so-called Διὸς βουλή, which makes the begetting and birth of Helen and the Dioscuri even more linked with the underlying plot. Furthermore, the *Nostos* (or a variety of *Nostoi*) could be conceived as the closure of this plot by presenting different exceptions to its finite cause.

I would cautiously conclude that the complex assemblage of interdependent motifs analyzed in this study, mediated as they were by means of a shared linguistic and poetic tradition in early Greek and Vedic society, could in fact be derived from a more coherent narrative substructure. Although specific manifestations of this substructure have begun to develop independently, the structure still thrives in the formal features that allow us to reassemble the motifs. Taken as a whole, on the one hand, the substructure evokes a quasi-universal thematization of depopulation and the beginning of the human condition, which by no means has to be derived from a common ancestor. On the other hand, some unique facets of this general pattern seem so specific as to exclude both universality and pure accident. I am especially referring to the myth of Heaven's incest and the birth of the Indo-European Dioscuri, but also to the role of the Dioscuri as rescuers of seamen. If we take these motifs to constitute parts of a common Indo-European or Greco-Vedic heritage, we should also inquire whether they disclose some kind of contiguity.

If a story of depopulation lurks in the background, it could be argued that the soteriological status of the Dioscuri was a direct consequence of events and cirucumstances surrounding their begetting and birth. We can imagine a number of alternative scenarios in this regard, yet all of which should function as precedents of the different versions found in Greek and Vedic mythology.

A possible scenario could be delineated as follows: At the first stage, the human condition is devised and brought about by the Sky-god through some sort of moral transgression (incest, adultery, illegitimate nuptial procedures) involving his own daughter, the Dawn-goddess. At the second stage, the multiple offspring born as a direct or indirect consequence of the transgression consists of a mortal pair foredoomed to extinction and a divine pair destined to alleviate and counteract this condition.

In Vedic mythology, the narrative substructure has resolved into a number of discrete themes: aetiologies of sacrifice, legends about the safe return of distressed mortals through divine intervention, the story about a deluge involving the mortal child of the Dawn-goddess' substitute.

In Greek epic and mythography, on the other hand, the substructure is still kept together by the "Cyclic" tradition. This becomes particularly clear if we focus the extreme points in the narrative plot known as the "Trojan Cycle," according to which the birth of Helen and Achilles provokes a catastrophic course of events exhausted by the safe return and subsequent death of Odysseus.

The fabric of this final hypothesis consists of many delicate strands. As pointed out in the beginning of this study, however, my motive force in treating this complex tapestry of themes and topics has not been to reconstruct an original narrative. Rather, I have attempted to examine the roots of early literary traditions through the different means and layers of their mediation. Oral traditions are virtually unconceivable without internal variation and dynamics. Regrettably, the kind of "proto-texts" sometimes considered to initiate literary traditions often look surprisingly similar to the texts bringing such traditions to an end: the compilation of a final version, the exclusion of divergent and apocryphal readings, the reduction of a multivocal chorus to a textual solo performance. If there is anything that this study has sought to achieve beyond the analysis of singular details (where disagreement will undoubtedly prevail), it is to add some complexity to a prehistory that would otherwise appear forever lost or deceptively uniform.

# ABBREVIATIONS

AB *Aitareya Brāhmaṇa*

AV *Atharva Veda*

AVP *Atharva Veda Paippalāda*

Diels Herman Diels and Walther Kranz, *Die Fragmente der Vorsokratiker*, Zürich: Weidmann, 1951.

Dor. Doric

EWAia Manfred Mayrhofer, *Etymologisches Wörterbuch des Altindoarischen*. Heidelberg: Univärsitätsverlag C. Winter. 1986-1996.

Gr. Greek

IG Inscriptiones Gaecae

Iir. Indo-Iranian

JB *Jaiminīya Brāhmaṇa*

KBo *Keilschrifttexte aus Boghazköy*. Berlin: Mann. 1916-.

KUB *Keilschrifturkunden aus Boghazköy*. Berlin: Mann. 1921-.

LIMC *Lexicon Iconographicum Mythologiae Classicae*. Hans Christoph Ackermann, Jean-Robert Gisler (eds). Zürich: Artemis Verlag. 1981-1997.

| | |
|---|---|
| Lith. | Lithuanian |
| LIV | Helmut Rix et al. (eds), *Lexikon der indogermanischen Verben*. Wiesbaden: Dr. Ludvig Reichert Verlag. 1998. |
| L-P | Denys Page and Edgar Lobel, *Poetarum Lesbiorum Fragmenta*, Oxford: Clarendon Press, 1963. |
| LSJ | Henry George Liddell and Robert Scott. *A Greek-English Lexicon*. Revised an augmented throughout by Sir Henry Stuart Jones with the assistance of Roderick McKenzie. Oxford: Claredon Press. 1968. |
| MS | *Maitrāyaṇī Saṃhitā* |
| OHG | Old High German |
| PGmc. | Proto-Germanic |
| PIE | Proto-Indo-European |
| PMG | Denys L. Page. *Poetarum Melici Graeci*. Oxford: Clarendon Press. 1962 |
| Pre-PGr. | Pre-Proto-Greek |
| Pre-PII | Pre-Proto-Indo-Iranian |
| RE | August Friedrich von Pauly and Georg Wissowa (eds), *Paulys Realencyclopaedie der classischen Altertumswissenschaft*. Stuttgart: J. B. Metzler, 1894-1972. |

| | |
|---|---|
| RV | *Rig Veda* |
| SEG | *Supplementum Epigraphicum Graecum*. Leyden: Sijthoff and Noordhoff. |
| ŚB | *Śatapatha Brāhmaṇa* |
| TB | *Taittirīya Brāhmaṇa* |
| TS | *Taittirīya Saṃhitā* |
| Ved. | Vedic |
| Y | *Yasna* |
| Yt. | *Yašt* |
| > | becomes |
| < | derives from |
| * | reconstructed form |

# BIBLIOGRAPHY

Allen, T. W., Halliday, W. R., and Sikes, E. E. 1963. *The Homeric Hymns*. Oxford: Oxford University Press.

Austin, Norman. 1994. *Helen of Troy and Her Shameless Phantom*. Ithaca: Cornell University Press.

Bloomfield, Maurice. 1893. "The Marriage of Saraṇyū, Tvaṣṭṛ's Daughter." Journal of the American Oriental Society 15.172-188.

Boedeker, Deborah Dickmann. 1974. *Aphrodite's Entry into Greek Epic*. Leiden: E. J. Brill.

Bowra, C. M. 1961. *Greek Lyric Poetry: From Alcman to Simonides. Second Revised Edition*. Oxford: Oxford University Press.

Burgess, Jonathan S. 2001. *The Tradition of the Trojan War in Homer & the Epic Cycle*. Baltimore: The Johns Hopkins University Press.

Calame, Claude. 1977. *Les chœurs de jeunes filles en Grècque archaïque*. Rome: Edizioni dell'ateneo & bizzarri.

Campbell, David A. 1982. *Greek Lyric I: Sappho and Alcaeus*. Cambridge, Mass.: Harvard University Press.

Catlin, Hector W. and Cavanagh, Helen. 1976. "Two Inscribed Bronzes from the Menelaion, Sparta." Kadmos. Zeitschrift für vor- und frühgriechische Epigraphik. 15.145-157.

Chantraine, Pierre. 1968. *La formation des noms en grec ancien*. Paris: Éditions Klincksieck.

Clader, Linda Lee. 1976. *Helen: The Evolution from Divine to Heroic in Greek Epic Tradition*. Leiden: E. J. Brill.

Crönert, Wilhelm. 1901. "Literarische Texte mit Ausschluß der christlichen." Archiv für Papyrusforschung 1.104-120.

Debrunner, Albert. 1917. *Griechische Wortbildungslehre.* Heidelberg: Carl Winters Universitätsbuchhandlung.

Deoudi, Maria. 1999. *Heroenkulte in homerischer Zeit.* BAR International Series 806. Oxford: Archaeopress.

Darmesteter, James. 1878 (= 1968). "Eine grammatikalische Metapher des Indogermanischen." In Schmitt, Rüdiger (ed./tr.) 1968.

Dumézil, Georges. 1948. *Mitra-Varuna. Essai sur deux representations indo-européennes de la souverainité.* Paris: Gallimard.

Dumézil, Georges. 1966. *Religion romaine archaique, avec un appendice sur la religion Étrusques.* Paris: Payot.

Dunkel, George. 1990. "Vater Himmels Gattin." Die Sprache 34.1-26.

Durante, Marcello. 1958 (= 1968), "Epea pteroenta. Die Rede als 'Weg' in griechischen und vedischen Bildern." In Schmitt, Rüdiger (ed./tr.) 1968.

Estell, Michael. 1999. "Orpheus and R̥bhu Revisited." Journal of Indo-European Studies 27.327-333.

EWAia = Mayrhofer, Manfred. *Etymologisches Wörterbuch des Altindoarischen.* Heidelberg: Universitätsverlag C. Winter. 1986-1996.

Farnell, Lewis Richard. 1921. *Greek Hero Cults and Ideas of Immortality.* Oxford: Oxford Unversity Press.

Forssman, Bernhard. 1993. "Lateinisch *ieiunus* und *ieientare.*" In J. Bendahman et. al. (ed.). *Indogermanica et Italica.* Festschrift für Helmut Rix zum 65. Geburtstag. Innsbruck: Innsbrucker Beiträge zur Sprachwissenschaft.

Fowler, R. L. 1987. *The Nature of Early Greek Lyric: Three Preliminary Studies.* Totonto: University of Toronto Press.

Frame, Douglas. 1978. *The Myth of Return in early Greek Epic*, New Haven and London: Yale University Press.

Frame, Douglas. Forthcoming. *Hippota Nestor.*

Garzya, Antonio. 1954. *Alcmane. I Frammenti. Testo critico, traduzione, commentario.* Napoli: S. Viti.

Geldner, Karl Friedrich. 1951. *Der Rig-Veda. Aus dem Sanskrit ins Deutsche übersetzt und mit einem laufenden Kommentar versehen.* Cambridge, Mass.: Harvard University Press.

Gemoll, Albert. 1886. *Die homerische Hymnen.* Leipzig: Teubner.

Gerhard, E. 1840. *Etruskische Spiegel* I. Berlin.

Gonda, Jan. 1986. *Prajāpati's Rise to a Higher Rank.* Leiden: E. J. Brill.

Graef, Botho. 1886. "Peleus und Thetis." Jahrbuch des kaiserlich deutschen archäologischen Instituts 1.190-204.

Harry, J. E. 1905. *Aeschylus/Prometheus Bound—with Introduction, Notes, and Critical Appendix.* New York: American Book Company.

Jackson, Peter. 2002a. "Light from Distant Asterisks: Towards a Description of the Indo-European Religious Heritage." Numen 49.61-102.

Jackson, Peter. 2002b. *Verbis pingendis: Contributions to the Study of Ritual Speech and Mythopoeia.* Innsbruck: Innsbrucker Beiträge zur Sprachwissenschaft.

Jackson, Peter and Oettinger, Norbert. 2003. "Traitana und Θraēta(o)na. Reste urindoiranischer Heldenlegenden." Indo-Iranian Journal 45.221-229.

Jackson, Peter. 2006. "The Poetics of Myth in Pindar's *Olympian* 9,47-49" in Georges Pinaul and Daniel Petit (eds), *La Langue poétique indo-européenne*, Leuven and Paris: Peeters. 125-132.

Jamison, Stephanie W. 1991. *The Ravenous Hyenas and the Wounded Sun: Myth and Ritual in Ancient India.* Ithaca: Cornell University Press.

Jamison, Stephanie W. 1997. "Formulaic Elements in Vedic Myth." In M. Witzel (ed.), *Inside the Texts / Beyond the Texts: New Approaches to the Study of the Vedas*. Columbia, Mo.: South Asia Books. 126-138.

Jamison, Stephanie W. 2001. "The Rigvedic Svayṃavara? Formulaic Evidence." In K. Karttunen and P. Koskikallio (eds), *Vidyārṇavavandanam. Essays in Honor of Asko Parpola*. Helsinki. 303-315.

Janda, Michael. 2000. *Eleusis. Das indogermanische Erbe der Mysterien*. Innsbruck. Innsbrucker Beiträge zur Sprachwissenschaft.

Janda, Michael. 2005. *Elysion. Entstehung und Entwicklung der griechischen Religion*. Innsbruck: Innsbrucker Beiträge zur Sprachwissenschaft.

Jurenka, Hugo. 1896. *Der Ägyptische Papyrus des Alkman*. Sitzungsberichte des kais. Akademie der Wissenschaften in Wien. Philosophisch-historische Klasse. Vol. 135. Wien: Buchhänder der kais. Akademie der Wissenschaften.

Kannicht, Richard. 1969. *Euripides Helena*. Vol. 2 (Kommentar). Heidelberg: Carl Winter.

Krieger, Xenia. 1975. *Der Kampf zwischen Peleus und Thetis in der griechischen Vasenmalerei. Eine typologische Untersuchung*. Westfällisches Wilhelm-Universität zu Münster (diss. photocopy).

Kuhn, Adalbert, "Die Herabunft des Feuers und Göttertranks" (1859), in Ernst Kuhn (ed.), *Mythologische Studien*, vol. 1, Gütersloh 1886.

Lawler, Lillian B. 1964. *The Dance in Ancient Greece*. London: Adam & Carles Black.

Lefkowiz, Mary R. 1993. "Seduction and Rape in Greek Myth." In Angelioki E. Laiou (ed.). *Consent and Coercion to Sex and Marriage in Ancient and Medieval Societies*. Washington, D.C.: Dumbarton Oaks Research Library Collection.

Lincoln, Bruce. 1999. *Theorizing Myth: Narrative, Ideology, and Scholarship*. Chicago: The Chicago University Press.

Malamoud, Charles. 1998. *Cooking the World: Ritual & Though in Ancient India.* Translated by David White. Oxford: Oxford University Press.

Mayer, Kenneth. 1996. "Helen and the Διὸς βουλή." American Journal of Philology 117.1-15.

Most, Glenn. 1987. "Alcman's 'Cosmogonic' Fragment (Fr. 5 Page, 81 Calame)." Classical Quarterly 37.1-19.

Mourelatos, Alexander, P. D. *The Route of Parmenides: A Study of Word, Image, and Argument in the Fragments.* New Haven and London: Yale University Press.

Nagy, Gregory. 1979. *The Best of the Achaeans: Concepts of the Hero in Archaic Greek Poetry.* Baltimore: The Johns Hopkins University Press.

Nagy, Gregory. 1990. *Greek Mythology and Poetics.* Ithaca: Cornell University Press.

Nagy, Gregory. 1996a. *Homeric questions.* Austin: Texas University Press.

Nagy, Gregory. 1996b. *Poetry as Performance: Homer and Beyond.* Cambridge: Cambridge University Press.

Narten, Johanna. 1960. "Das vedische Verbum *math.*" Indo-Iranian Journal 4.121-135.

Oettinger, Norbert. 1998. "Semantisches zu Pan, Pūṣan und Hermes." In Jay Jasanoff, H. Craig Melchert and L. Olivers (ed.). *Mír Curad. Studies in Honor of Calvert Watkins.* Innsbruck: Innsbrucker Beiträge zur Sprachwissenschaft. 539-548.

Oettinger, Norbert. 1999. "Zum nordwest-indogermanischen Lexikon (mit einer Bemerkung zum hethitischen Genitiv auf *-l*)." In Peter Anreiter and Erzsébet Jerem (ed.). *Studia celtica et indogermanica. Festschrift für Wolfgang Meid zum 70. Geburtstag.* Budapest.

Page, Denys L. 1951. *Alcman: The Partheineion.* Oxford: Oxford University Press.

Pisani, Vittore 1928. "Elena e εἴδωλον." Rivista de Filologia e Istruzione Classica. 56.476-499. Reprinted in Vittore Pisani. 1969. *Lingue e Culture*. Brescia: Editrice Paideia. 325-345

Risch, Ernst. 1987. "Die Älteste Zeugnisse für κλέος ἄφθιτον." Zeitschrift für Vergleichende Sprachforschung 100.3-11.

Robson, J. E. 1997. "Bestiality and Bestial Rape in Greek Myth." In Susan Deacy and Karen F. Pierce (ed.). *Rape in Antiquity*. Swansea: The Classical Press of Wales.

Schmitt, Rudiger. 1967. *Dichtung und Dichtersprache in indogermanischer Zeit*. Wiesbaden: Otto Harrasowitz.

Schmitt, Rüdiger (ed./tr.). 1968. *Indogermanische Dichtersprache*. Darmstadt: Wissenschaftliche Buchgesellschaft.

Schweizer-Keller, R. 1972. *Von Umgang des Aischylos mit der Sprache. Interpretationen zu seinem Namendeutungen*. Zürich: Arau.

Simon, Erika. c.1975. *Pergamon und Hesiod*. Mainz am Rhein: P. von Zabern.

Skutsch, Otto. 1987. "Helen, Her Name and Nature." Journal of Hellenic Studies. 107.188-192.

Slatkin, Laura. 1991. *The Power of Thetis: Allusion and Interpretation in the* Iliad. Berkeley and Los Angeles: University of California Press.

Smith, Jonathan Z. 1990. *Drudgery Divine: On the Comparison of Early Christianities and the Religions of Late Antiquity*. Chicago: The University of Chicago Press.

Starke, Frank. 1997. "Troia im Kontext des historisch-politischen Umfeldes Kleinasiens im 2. Jahrtausend." Studia Troica 7.447-487.

Steets, Cheryl. 1993. *The Sun maiden's wedding: An Indo-European sunrise/sunset myth*. University of California, Los Angeles (diss. photocopy).

Szemerényi, Oswald. 1971. Review of Pierre Chantraine, *Dictionaire étymologique de la langue grecque — Histoire des mots. Tome I: A-Δ, 1968; Tome II: E-K,* 1970. Paris: Klincksieck. XVIII, 305. 307-607 S. 68; 76F. *Gnomon* 43.641-675.

Wackernagel, Jacob. 1916. *Sprachliche Untersuchungen zu Homer.* Göttingen: Vandenhoek & Ruprecht.

Watkins, Calvert. 1970. "Studies in Indo-European legal language, institutions, and mythology." In G. Cardona et al. (ed.). *Indo-European and Indo-Europeans.* 321-354. Philadelphia: Unversity of Pensylvania Press.

Watkins, Calvert, 1986. "The Language of the Trojans." In Machtheld J. Mellink (ed.). *Troy and the Trojan War.* 45-62. Bryn Mawr: Bryn Mawr University Press.

Watkins, Calvert. 1995. *How to Kill a Dragon: Aspects of Indo-European Poetics.* New York: Oxford University Press.

Welcker, Friedrich Gottlieb. 1849. *Der epische Cyclus oder die homerischen Dichter. Zweiter Teil.* Bonn: Eduard Weber.

Weber, Albrecht. 1885. *Indische Studien. Beiträge für die Kunde des indischen Altherthums.* 18 vols. Leipzig: F. A. Brockhaus.

West. Martin L. 1966. *Hesiod: Theogony.* Oxford: Clarendon Press.

West, Martin L. 1988. "The Rise of the Greek epic." Journal of Hellenic Studies 108.151-172.

Wikander, Stig. 1957. "Nakula et Sahadeva." Orientalia Suecana. 6.66-96.

INDEX OF PASSAGES


**Anatolian**

| | | |
|---|---|---|
| KBo | 4.112,46 | 31 |
| KUB | 35.102 | 31 |

**Indic**

| | | |
|---|---|---|
| AB | 3,33 | 68-69 |
| | 3,34,1 | 71 |
| AV | 7,10,2 | 15 |
| | 9,3,18 | 20 |
| | 13,3,13 | 20 |
| | 18,1,53 | 73 |
| | 18,2,33 | 73 |
| AVP | 2,72,2 (= 2,80,2) | 20 |
| Bṛhaddevatā | 4,21 | 76 |
| | 6,33-7,6 | 76 |
| | 7,5 | 76 |
| JB | 3,262-263 | 69, 70 |
| Mahābhārata (Vanap.) | 12747-12802 | 114 |
| MS | 4,2,12 | 68 |
| | 3,6,5 | 68-69 |
| RV | 1,25,5 | 22 |
| | 1,25,13 | 20 |
| | 1,30,20 | 79 |
| | 1,50,9 | 105 |
| | 1,53,1 | 78 |
| | 1,58,8 | 58 |
| | 1,71,5 | 64, 66, 70 |
| | 1,71,8 | 71 |
| | 1,96,3 | 58 |
| | 1,112-121 | 103 |
| | 1,112,6.20 | 104 |
| | 1,116,3-5 | 104-105, 108 |
| | 1,116,17 | 73 |
| | 1,117,14-15 | 104 |
| | 1,117,15 | 107 |
| | 1,119,4 | 105-106 |
| | 1,119,4.8 | 104 |
| | 1,139,1 | 78 |
| | 1,142,10 | 67 |
| | 1,158 | 102 |
| | 1,158,3 | 104 |
| | 1,164,3 | 18 |
| | 1,164,33 | 65-66 |
| | 1,180,1-2 | 62 |
| | 1,181,1 | 58 |
| | 1,181,4 | 58, 61 |
| | 1,182,1 | 58 |
| | 1,182,5 | 105 |
| | 1,184,5-7 | 104 |
| | 2,4,6 | 23 |
| | 2,7,6 | 58 |
| | 2,12,13 | 75 |
| | 2,15,7 | 83 |
| | 2,31,1-4 | 13 |
| | 2,39,6 | 99 |
| | 2,41,7 | 99 |
| | 3,4,9 | 67 |
| | 3,31,1-3 | 64 |
| | 3,39,1-3 | 59 |
| | 3,39,3 | 60, 73, 80 |
| | 3,55,19 | 67 |
| | 3,58,1 | 60 |
| | 4,1,10 | 18 |
| | 4,1,13 | 71 |
| | 4,30,8-11 | 81 |
| | 4,30,10 | 82 |
| | 4,30,11 | 82 |
| | 4,43,3 | 57, 59 |
| | 4,44,2 | 57 |
| | 4,53,2 | 67 |
| | 5,2,11 | 13 |
| | 5,15,3 | 71 |

| | | |
|---|---|---|
| | 5,42,13 | 66, 72, 79 |
| | 5,73,4 | 61 |
| | 6,12,4 | 64 |
| | 6,32,1 | 13 |
| | 6,70,3 | 67 |
| | 7,15,3 | 60 |
| | 7,34,22 | 66 |
| | 8,3,23 | 108 |
| | 8,25,19 | 66 |
| | 8,41,9 | 22 |
| | 9,5,9 | 67 |
| | 9,86,28 | 67 |
| | 9,91,5 | 12 |
| | 10,10,1 | 58 |
| | 10,14,5 | 78 |
| | 10,17,1-2 | 72-75, 77-78, 80, 82-83 |
| | 10,39,12 | 79 |
| | 10,40,12 | 60, 73 |
| | 10,46,9 | 66 |
| | 10,58,1 | 78 |
| | 10,61,4 | 71 |
| | 10,61,5-8 | 65 |
| | 10,61,7 | 67, 70 |
| | 10,61,8 | 67, 80, 82 |
| | 10,61,17 | 67 |
| | 10,61,23 | 73 |
| | 10,62,11 | 72-74, 115 |
| | 10,85,28-30 | 83 |
| | 10,138,5 | 82 |
| | 10,172,1 | 23, 82 |
| | Khila 2,1 | 108 |
| | Khila 11,5 | 73 |
| ŚB | 1,7,4,1-3 | 68-69 |
| | 1,7,4,3-4 | 67 |
| | 1,8,1-10 | 114 |
| TB | 1,7,10,1 | 20 |
| TS | 2,1.7 | 20 |
| | 5,6,21 | |
| | 6,4,8 | 20 |

| | | |
|---|---|---|
| Yāska | 12,1 | 61 |

**Iranian**

| | | |
|---|---|---|
| Y | 9,4 | 79 |
| | 44,3 | 18 |
| Yt. | 5,61ff. | 104 |
| | 13,2-3 | 20 |
| Vīdēvdāt | 2,21.43 | 114 |

**Greek**

| | | |
|---|---|---|
| Aeschylus | | |
| *Agam.* | 687 | 88 |
| *Hiket.* | 206 | 18 |
| *Prom.* | 935 | 38 |
| Alciphron | | |
| *Ep.* | 1,33 | 38 |
| Alcaeus | Fr. B2, 3 (L-P) | 107 |
| | Fr. B2, 5-8 (L-P) | 101 |
| | Fr. B2, 9 (L-P) | 101 |
| | Fr. B2, 11-12 (L-P) | |
| 101 | | |
| | Fr. B2, 34 (L-P) | 102 |
| Alcman | Fr. 1 (PMG) | 48ff. |
| | Fr. 1, 85 | 49 |
| | Fr. 5 (PMG) | 42 |
| Apollodorus | | |
| *Lib.* | 3,10,7 | 34 |
| Archilochus | | |
| | Fr. 131 (West) | 19 |
| Aristophanes | | |
| *Lysistrata* | 1308-15 | 49 |
| Callimachus | | |
| *Hymn to Artemis* | 232 | 38 |

| | | |
|---|---|---|
| Critias | | |
| *Sisyphus* | 33 | 20 |
| Democritus | Fr. 30 (Diels) | 18 |
| Diodours Siculus | 4,67,2 | 40 |
| (= *Diod.*) | | |
| Epic Cycle | | |
| *Cypria* | Fr. 1 (Davies) | 42, 112 |
| | Fr. 2 (Davies) | 43 |
| | Fr. 6 (Davies) | 61 |
| | Fr. 7 (Davies) | 36-37 |
| Euripides | | |
| *Hel.* | 16-22 | 35 |
| | 31 | 86 |
| | 257-9 | 35 |
| | 1451-1511 | 102 |
| | 1465-1466 | 49 |
| | 1642ff. | 101 |
| | 1664-1665 | 102, 115 |
| *Ion* | 136 | 18 |
| | 1078ff. | 43 |
| *Iph. Aul.* | 49-51 | 35 |
| | 70-71 | 89 |
| | 794-800 | 35 |
| | 1055 | 43 |
| *Iph. Taur.* | 427ff. | 43 |
| *Rhes.* | 342 | 38 |
| Eustathius | 1796 | 95 |
| Herodot | 2,112-120 | 85 |
| | 5,75 | 41 |
| | 7,191 | 44 |
| Hesiod | | |
| *Catalogue of Women* | Fr 204 (MW) | 113 |
| *Op.* | 45 | 25 |
| (= *Works and Days*) | | |
| | 252-53 | 20 |

| | | |
|---|---|---|
| | 514-516 | 15 |
| | 727 | 15 |
| *Shield of Heracles* | 275-277 | 48 |
| *Theog.* | 128 | 22 |
| | 176 | 19 |
| | 213 | 35 |
| | 223-24 | 35 |
| | 371-47 | 53 |
| | 592 | 38 |
| Homer | | |
| *Il.* | 3,50-51 | 38 |
| | 3,238 | 35 |
| | 3,391-394 | 46 |
| | 3,394 | 48 |
| *Od.* | 1,326 | 95 |
| | 3,132 | 108 |
| | 3,160 | 108 |
| | 4,227 | 53 |
| | 4,349-570 | 86 |
| | 4,586 | 102 |
| | 5,37 | 102 |
| | 7,36 | 107 |
| | 8,73 | 96 |
| | 8,260 | 48 |
| | 8,555.63 | 106 |
| | 11,235ff. | 40 |
| | 11,260ff. | 40 |
| | 11,298 | 35, 41 |
| | 12,1-4 | 45 |
| | 12,419 | 108 |
| | 13,53 | 102 |
| | 14.309 | |
| | 15, 251-252 | 46 |
| | 18,136f. | 19 |
| | 19,290 | 102 |
| | 23,315 | 102 |
| | 23,340 | 102 |
| Homeric Hymns | | |
| *To Aphrodite* (5) | 117-118 | 45 |
| | 200-201 | 46 |
| | 218-219 | 46 |

| | | |
|---|---|---|
| | 235 | 46 |
| *To the Dioscuri* (33) | 1-2 | 98 |
| | | 100, 102 |
| Pausanias | 2,22,6 | 38, 84 |
| | 4,16,9 | 45 |
| | 7,5,3 | 34 |
| | 10,5,8 | 13 |
| Photius | | |
| *Bibliotheca* | 149a | 45f. |
| Pindar | | |
| *Ol.* | 9,47-49 | 12 |
| | 9,47 | 60 |
| | 1,110-111 | 13 |
| *Pyth.* | 3,112-114 | 13 |
| | 4,246-248 | 12 |
| | 8,95-96 | 19 |
| | 9,104 | 60 |
| *Nem.* | 6,53-54 | 11f. |
| | 10,21 | 60 |
| | 10,79ff. | 61 |
| | 10,80 | 34 |
| *Isth.* | 5,63 | 12 |
| Fr. | 6a | 60 |
| Plato | | |
| *Phaedrus* | 242a | 85 |
| *Republic* | 9.586c | 85 |
| Plutarch | | |
| *Theseus* | 31,2 | 45 |
| Sappho | Fr. 166 (PMG) | 35 |
| Stesichorus | Fr. 192 (PMG) | 84 |
| | Fr. 208-209 | 95 |
| Terpander | Fr. 4 (PMG) | 100 |
| Theocritus | | |
| *Epithalamium for Helen* | 18,2-3 | 51 |
| | 18,8 | 51 |
| | 18,26-28 | 51 |
| | 18,38-48 | 51 |


**Latin**


| | | |
|---|---|---|
| Aelius Aristides | | |
| *Orationes* | 1,128 | 85 |
| Ennius | | |
| *Annales* | 120 | 18 |
| Himerius | | |
| *Eclogue* | XIII,21 | 43 |
| Hygin | | |
| *Fabulae* | 186 | 41 |

INDEX OF WORDS


**Proto-Indo-European**

**deiu̯ós* 22
**di̯eu̯ ph$_2$tér* (voc.) 17
*√*di̯éu̯* 22
**di̯éu̯s* 18, 22
**diu̯ós dugh$_2$tér* 23
**diu̯ós népoth$_1$e* 90
**diu̯ós suHnúh$_1$* 56
**dugh$_2$tér (*diu̯ós)* 23
**ǵénh$_1$tōr* (**ph$_2$tḗr*) 17-18
**ghos(-ti-)* 15
**ghs-* 15
*√*g$^{wh}$en (*persó-)* 92
**Hiaǵ-i̯u-* 59
*√*Hiaǵ* 60
*√*Hu̯er* 21
**h$_1$eḱu̯o-* 98
**h$_1$gé-h$_1$gr̥-* 60
*√*h$_1$ger* 60
*√*h$_2$elk* 99
**h$_2$eu̯sōs* 22-23, 89, 93
*√*h$_2$leks* 99
*√*h$_2$u̯es* 79
*√h$_3$mei̯ǵ (*u̯r̥Hdhu̯os)* 15
**h$_3$r̥bhéu-* 24
**ḱléu̯os* 14
**ḱléu̯os ń̥dg$^{w}$hitom* 14
**naus* 106
*√*nes* 96-97, 99, 107
**-no-* 21
**nosos* 99, 107
**nostó-* 107-108
**nstó-* 108
**persó- (√*g$^{wh}$en)* 92
**ph$_2$tḗr *ǵénh$_1$tōr* 17-18
**promāth$_2$eu̯-* 24
**sédos* 22
*√*sel* 86-88, 93
**seleneh$_2$* 86, 88-89, 93
**seleni̯uh$_2$* (Pre-PII) 86, 93
**su̯eleneh$_2$* (Pre-PGr.) 88
*√smei̯* 23
*√*teḱþ* 14
*√*tetḱ* 14, 24
*√*tu̯eis* 64
**u̯aǵro-* 24
**u̯ék$^{w}$os (√*tetḱ)* 14
*√*u̯el* 21
*√*u̯elh$_1$* 89
**u̯énos* 23, 82
*√*u̯er* 21
**u̯érH-* 22
**u̯eruno-* 21-22
*√*u̯es* 79
**u̯oru-* 21
**u̯oruno-* 21
**u̯r̥Hdhu̯os (√h$_3$mei̯ǵ)* 15

**Indic**

*ájahād* 73-74, 77
*ádhi√skandh* 67
*apagohá-* 83
*ápas* 21
*abhi√dhay* 70
*aśvin-* 57, 98
*ásūta* 74
*ástam* 105, 108-109
*ātmán* 105
*ātmanvát* 105
*ā́pas* 21
*ā́sit* 74
*ukṣaṇyá-* 80
*ukṣaṇyánt-* 80
*ukṣaṇyú-* 80
*usr̥̄́-* 64
*ū́rjaḥ putrám* 58
*ū́rjo nápāt* 58
*ūrdhvó mekṣyāmi* 15

*√jan* 67, 83
*janitár-* 18, 83
*√jar* 60, 64
*jā́gr̥-* 60
*jā́gr̥vi-* 59-60
*jārá-* 63
*√takṣ* 13
*tū́ripa-* 66
*tvíṣi-* 64
*√tveṣ* 64
*dāsá-* 104
*divá ā́jātā* 57, 59
*divá(s) duhitár-* 53
*dívo nápāta* 56-57, 59, 115
*duhitár- divás* 53
*dyáv-* 66
*√dyut* 18
*dyáus (pitár)* 17
*dyaúṣ pitā́ janitā́* 18
*dvā́ mithunā́* 73
*dhruvám̩ sádaḥ* 22
*nápāt-* 58
*návyase ... sūktā́ya* 12
*nás-* 76
*√nas* 57, 107
**nas-ati-* 57, 62, 107
*na-ša-ti-i̯a-an-na* Mitt. Aryan 107
*nā́satya-* 57, 62, 76, 98-99
*ni√vah* 105
*náu-* 106
*parā√pat* 70
*pitár* 17, 83
*pitŕ̥bhya* 106
*putrā́ divás* 59
*pra√jan* 67, 83
*prajā́-* 70
*prajā́pati-* 67
*budhná* 60
*√bodh* 60
*√bhar* 62
*√math* 24
*mathnā́ti* 24
*mánojavas-* 107
*mithuná-* 60
*yajati* 59
*yamásya mātā́* 74
*√rakṣ* 99
*rakṣitā́rā* 99
*vácas-* 13
*vánas-* 23, 82
*varu-* 21
*váruṇa-* 21, 24
*váruṇaṃ ... urucákṣam* 22
*várūtā* 21
*varūtŕ̥* 21
*vas-atí-* 62, 107
*vāsātya-* 62
*√vas*$^2$ 62, 79
*√vas*$^3$ 62
*√vah ástam* 108
*vípra-* 104
*vīryà* 75
*vai* 70
*śaraṇe divo* 66
*śrávo ... ákṣitam* 14
*sádaḥ (dhruvám̩)* 22
*√sar* 73, 80-83, 86
*sárat* 80-81
*saraṇyá-* 80
*saraṇyú-* 73, 80
*saraṇyū́-* 73, 80, 83, 86
*sávarṇa-* 72
*sasā́ra* 81
*sáhasas putró* 58
*suśaraṇá-* 66, 86
*sūno sahaso* 58
*sūnū́ divás* 59
*sū́ras duhitár-* 57
*sū́rasya duhitár-* 57
*stómataṣṭa-* 59
*spáśas* 20
*svayaṃvara* 89

*sváyukta-* 105
*sváyukti-* 105
*ha* 70

**Iranian**

*√taš* 14
*nå̄ŋhaiθiia* 107
*pauriio mašiiō* 79
*barəθri-* 62
*vacah-* 13
*vacastašti-* 13
*vifra-* 104
*ząθa patā* 18

**Armenian**

*tiw* 18

**Greek**

᾿Αγέλαος 98
αἱρέω 45, 55, 88
*a-qi-ti-ta* Myc. 14
ἅζομαι 60
αλέξω 99
ἀλκή 99
ἀλκί 99
ἀναιρέω 45
῎Ανακε 102
᾿Ανάκεια 102
ἅρμα 13
*(h)armo-* Myc. 13
ἁρμόζω 13
ἁρπασθῆναι 45
**Arkhelawos* Myc. 98
ἄσμενος 96
ἀστερόεις 21
ἀσφαλὲς ἕδος 22
᾿Αχαιοί 28
῎Αωι 52
᾿Αώς 50
᾿Αώτι (dat.) 49
᾿Αώτις 52
γεννήτορ (Ζεύς) 18
Διὸς βουλή 42, 111, 115
Διὸς θυγάτηρ 53-54
ΔιϜὸς κώροιν μεγάλοιο 100
Διὸς παῖς 36f.
Διὸς ὗιε 56
Διόσκουροι 56
δρόμος 51-52
ἐγείρω 60
ἕδος (ἀσφαλές) 22
εἴδωλον 85-86
ἐλάνη 88
ἐλεῖν 88
᾿Ελένη 86
ἐλένη 88
Ηελε[να] (?) 87
Ϝελέναι (dat.) 87
ἔνδιος 18
(Ϝ)έπος 13
ἐπέων τέκτονες 13
*ἐρανός 21
εὐδία 18
εὔιπποι 57
εὔνοος θυμός 107
εὔπλοια 102
ἐχυρός 21
θυγάτηρ Διός 53
Ζεῦ πάτερ (voc.) 17
*Ϝίλιος 28
*wi-pi-no-* Myc. 96
ἵπποτα 98
ἱππόται σοφοί 57
᾿Ιφίνος 96
κάνναθρα 52
κλέα ἀνδρῶν 96
κλέος ἄφθιτον 14
Κλεόξενος 14
λέγω 96
λευκόπωλοι 57
λόγος 96
μαρμαρυγάς 43

| | |
|---|---|
| ναῦς | 106 |
| **Nehelawos* | 98 |
| νέον ... ὕμνον | 12 |
| νέμεσις | 38, 54 |
| νέομαι | 96-97 |
| νόος | 96-97 |
| -νόος | 96 |
| νόστος | 95-97, 108 |
| ξένος | 15 |
| ὁδὸν ἀμαξιτόν | 12 |
| ὄζος Ἄρηος | 61 |
| ὀρθὸς ὀμείχειν | 15 |
| ὀρανός | 21 |
| ὄρθριος | 51 |
| οὐρανός | 21, 24 |
| οὐρανός εὐρυς | 22 |
| ὀχυρός | 21 |
| πάτρα | 105-106 |
| πατήρ | 17, 37 |
| πατήρ (γενέτορ) | 18 |
| προσηῷα | 50 |
| πῆμα | 38, 42 |
| Προμαθεύς | 24 |
| πωλία | 49 |
| πῶλοι | 49 |
| σωτῆρες | 100 |
| √τεκτ | 14 |
| ὑμέναιος | 51 |
| φέβομαι | 96 |
| φόβος | 96 |
| χοραγός | 49 |
| χορέω | 43 |
| χορηγός | 49 |
| χορός | 41-48, 55 |
| χῶρος | 44, 55 |

**Illyrian (?)**

| | |
|---|---|
| Δειπάτυρος | 17 |

**Italic**

| | |
|---|---|
| *diēs* | 18 |
| *genitor (pater)* | 18 |
| *iaiientāre* | 59 |
| *iouios puclois* | 56 |
| *Iupater* Umb. | 17 |
| *Iuppiter* | 17 |
| *genitor (pater)* | 18 |
| *Venus* | 23 |
| *dominus* | 21 |

**Etruscan**

| | |
|---|---|
| Ϝλεμab[α] | 87 |
| Θesan | 54 |

**Germanic**

| | |
|---|---|
| *HlewagastiR* Run. | 14 |
| **Tīwaz* PGmc. | 22 |
| **Wōðanaz* PGmc. | 22 |
| *swellen* OHG | 88 |

**Lithuanian**

| | |
|---|---|
| *diẽva sūnẽlai* | 56 |
| *svelù* | 88 |

**Latvian**

| | |
|---|---|
| *dieva dēli* | 56 |

# MÜNCHENER STUDIEN ZUR SPRACHWISSENSCHAFT

Alle Hefte tragen die ISSN 0077-1910.
Nachstehend nicht aufgeführte sind vergriffen!

MSS 62 – 2002 [2006]
302 S., Brosch., ca. EUR 48,-
MSS 61 – 2001
176 S., Brosch., EUR 33,-
MSS 60 – 2000
176 S., Brosch., EUR 33,-
MSS 59 – 1999
176 S., Brosch., EUR 28,-
MSS 58 – 1998
176 S., Brosch., EUR 28,-
MSS 57 – 1997
220 S., Brosch., EUR 28,-
MSS 56 – 1996
192 S., Brosch., EUR 28,-
MSS 55 – 1994 [1995]
176 S., Brosch., EUR 25,-
MSS 54 – 1993 [1994]
276 S., Brosch., EUR 25,-
MSS 53 – 1992 [1994]
204 S., Brosch., EUR 22,50
MSS 52 – 1991
184 S., Brosch.,EUR 20,-
MSS 51 – 1990
253 S., Brosch., EUR 25,-
MSS 50 – 1989
223 S., Brosch., EUR 22,50
MSS 46 – 1985
252 S., Brosch., EUR 15,-

MSS 42 – 1983
243 S., Brosch., EUR 20,-
MSS 40 – 1981
227 S., Brosch., EUR 16,-
MSS 39 – 1980
202 S., Brosch., EUR 17,-
MSS 37 – 1978
177 S., Brosch., EUR 15,-
MSS 33 – 1975
114 S., Brosch., EUR 15,-
MSS 32 – 1974
Brosch., EUR 15,-
MSS 31 – 1973
172 S., Brosch., EUR 15,-
MSS 29 – 1971
196 S., Brosch., EUR 15,-
MSS 28 – 1970
142 S., Brosch., EUR 15,-
MSS 27 – 1969
126 S., Brosch., EUR 15,-
MSS 26 – 1970
108 S., Brosch., EUR 15,-
MSS 20 – 1967
96 S., Brosch., EUR 15,-
MSS 19 – 1966
157 S., Brosch., EUR 15,-
MSS 4 – 1954
65 S., Brosch., EUR 15,-

MÜNCHENER STUDIEN ZUR SPRACHWISSENSCHAFT

– Beihefte der neuen Folge –

Joachim Matzinger
**Untersuchungen zum altarmenischen Nomen**
*Die Flexion des Substantivs*
*MSS Beiheft 22*
166 S., Brosch.; EUR 27,-
ISBN 3-89754-108-4

Hisashi Miyakawa
**Die altindischen Grundzahlwörter im Rigveda**
*MSS Beiheft 21*
296 Seiten, Brosch.; EUR 40,-
ISBN 3-89754-227-7

Berthold Forssman
**Lettische Grammatik**
*MSS Beiheft 20*
418 Seiten, Hardc.; EUR 50,-
ISBN 3-89754-194-7

Almut Hintze, Eva Tichy (Hg.)
**Anusantatyai**
*MSS Beiheft 19*
345 S., Brosch.; EUR 40,-
ISBN 3-89754-181-5

Michael Janda
**Über „Stock und Stein“**
Die indogermanischen Variationen eines universalen Phraseologismus
*MSS Beiheft 18*
210 S., Brosch.; EUR 28,-
ISBN 3-927522-29-5

Jared S. Klein
**On Personal Deixis in Classical Armenian**
A Study of the Syntax and Semantics of the n-, s-, and d- Demonstratives
in Manuscripts E and M of the Old Armenian Gospels
*MSS Beiheft 17*
146 S., Brosch.; EUR 25,-
ISBN 3-927522-24-4

Ekaterini Tzamali
**Syntax und Stil bei Sappho**
*MSS Beiheft 16*
550 S., Brosch.; EUR 50,-
ISBN 3-927522-23-6

MÜNCHENER STUDIEN ZUR SPRACHWISSENSCHAFT

– Beihefte der alten Folge –

Wolfgang Schlachter
**Studien zum Wachstum des Wortschatzes an skandinavischen und finnischen Lehnadjektiva**
*MSS Beiheft A (1952) – Rev. Nachdruck 1962*
105 S., Brosch.; EUR 15,-
ISBN 3-927522-16-3

Julius Forssman
**Skandinavische Spuren in der altrussischen Sprache und Dichtung**
*Hg. Bernhard Forssman*
*MSS Beiheft L – 2. Aufl. 1983*
116 S., Brosch.; EUR 15,-
ISBN 3-927522-64-3

Ferdinand Sommer
Hg. Bernhard Forssman
**Schriften aus dem Nachlaß**
*MSS Beiheft 1 – 1977*
XIV + 392 S., Ganzleinen;
EUR 22,50
ISBN 3-927522-10-4

Wolfgang Benzing
**Konkurrenz zwischen denominativem Adjektiv und Kompositum im Deutschen**
*MSS Beiheft 3 – 1968*
240 S., Brosch.; EUR 17,-
ISBN 3-927522-18-X

Georges Darms
**Schwäher und Schwager, Hahn und Huhn**
Die Vrddhi-Ableitung im Germanischen
*MSS Beiheft 9 – 1978*
XXXII + 568 S., Brosch.; EUR 25,-
ISBN 3-927522-20-1

Wolfgang Griepentrog
**Synopse der gotischen Evangelientexte**
*MSS Beiheft 14 – 1988*
171 S., Brosch.; EUR 15,-
ISBN 3-927522-11-2

# VERGLEICHENDE SPRACHWISSENSCHAFT

Joachim Matzinger
**Der altalbanische Text Mbsuame e krështerë (Dottrina cristiana) des Lekë Matrënga von 1592**
*Jenaer Indogermanistische Textbearbeitungen, Bd. 3*
X + 306 S., Brosch.; EUR 34,80
ISBN 3-89754-117-3

Max Deeg
**Die altindische Etymologie nach dem Verständnis Yāska's und seiner Vorgänger**
*Würzburger Studien zur Sprache & Kultur, Bd. 2*
436 S., Brosch.; EUR 50,-
ISBN 3-927522-05-8

Jost Gippert (Bearb.)
**Index Galenicus**
*Wortformindex zu den Schriften Galens*
1281 S., 2 Bände im Schuber, Leinen; EUR 200,-
ISBN 3-927522-09-0

Peter Kuhlmann
**Sappho**
Die größeren Fragmente des 1. Buches
*Jenaer Indogermanistische Textbearbeitungen, Bd. 2*
208 S., Brosch.; EUR 25,-
ISBN 3-89754-198-X

Rosemarie Lühr
**Die Gedichte des Skalden Egill**
*Jenaer Indogermanistische Textbearbeitungen, Bd. 1*
410 S., Brosch.; EUR 25,50
ISBN 3-89754-157-2

Yoko Nishina (Hg.)
**Europa et Asia Polyglotta**
Sprachen und Kulturen
244 S., Brosch.; EUR 35,-
ISBN 3-89754-125-4

Josef H. Röll
**Der Vikramacarita**
*Würzburger Studien zur Sprache & Kultur, Bd. 1*
199 S., Brosch. mit Fadenheft.; EUR 25,-
ISBN 3-927522-01-5

Bernfried Schlerath
**Das geschenkte Leben**
Erinnerungen und Briefe
309 S., Brosch.; EUR 20,50
ISBN 3-89754-165-3

Bernfried Schlerath
**Kleine Schriften**
XXXII + 778 S., 2 Bde. Hardc.; EUR 100,-
ISBN 3-89754-166-1

Isidor von Sevilla
**Über Glauben und Aberglauben**
*Etymologien, VIII. Buch, übersetzt von Dagmar Linhart*
91 S., Hardc.; EUR 15,50
ISBN 3-927522-25-2